Hunting and Trapping on the Upper Magalloway River and Parmachenee Lake

First Winter in the Maine Wilderness

By Capt. Fred C. Barker

and

J. S. Danforth

Published by Pantianos Classics

ISBN-13: 978-1-78987-280-4

First published in 1882

Contents

Dedication v

Preface vi

Chapter One - Up River 7

Chapter Two - Setting Traps 12

Chapter Three – Capturing a Caribou 17

Chapter Four - Making A Road to the North 20

Chapter Five - Under the Ice After Beaver 25

Chapter Six - More Caribou 28

Chapter Seven - Back to the Home Camp 30

Chapter Eight - Smoking Out a Fisher 33

Chapter Nine - The Fox without a Tail 36

Chapter Ten - Otter at Play 38

Chapter Eleven - The Avalanche 41

Chapter Twelve - Jared 45

Chapter Thirteen - The Big Snow Storm 47

Chapter Fourteen - Thirty-Five Degrees Below Zero 50

Chapter Fifteen - A Canal Dam 52

Chapter Sixteen - Farther into the Wilderness 55

Chapter Seventeen - The Mired Moose 58

Chapter Eighteen - Lookout Mountain 59

Chapter Nineteen - The Lynx Fight 64

Chapter Twenty - Gathering in the Traps 66

Chapter Twenty-One - Who's Afraid of a Lynx? 67

Chapter Twenty-Two - Moving Caribou Meat to Camp 70

Chapter Twenty-Three - A Ride on a Buck 72

Chapter Twenty-Four - A Night in the Woods 76

Chapter Twenty-Five - We Lose Our Hats 79

Chapter Twenty-Six - Preparing to Move 82

Chapter Twenty-Seven - A Bear Hunt 85

Chapter Twenty-Eight - Farewell to the Home Camp 88

Chapter Twenty-Nine - Return to Civilization 90

Dedication

TO OUR CITY FRIENDS WHO SPEND THEIR VACATIONS IN THE CANOE AND AROUND THE CAMP FIRE IN THE FORESTS OF MAINE,

THIS BOOK IS DEDICATED BY
Capt. F. C. Barker and J. S. Danforth.

Preface

During the long winter evenings in our home camp the second winter we spent in the Northern wilderness, we busied ourselves copying a journal which we kept the winter before, but with no idea of ever putting it before the public, nor the one we kept the second winter.

But when we saw so many writing about the woods and giving such flowery descriptions of the good times they had had, we thought we would have our book published, and give it to the people — a plain record of facts, without any change to make it into a romance.

We hope and trust that at least the people who know us as hunters, trappers and guides, will take it as it is, without criticism.

During the winter of 1882-3 we will publish a book entitled *Hunting and Trapping on the Upper Magalloway River and Parmachenee Lake: Barker and Danforth's Second Winter in the Wilderness.* The volume will contain three hundred pages, with illustrations, and will give an account of the scheme which worked to the preservation of the fish and game north of the Rangeley Lakes; also how we roughed it in order to learn the mighty forest.

F. C. B. & J. S. D.

Chapter One - Up River

AT ten o'clock in the forenoon, on October 10, 1876, we had our outfit piled on the steamboat landing at Errol, N. H.

It consisted of two boats; one a large Indian rock boat, capable of carrying one thousand pounds, the other a smaller one, built by Rushton, at Canton, N.Y., four hundred steel traps of different sizes, from the small, one-spring musk-rat trap, to the sixteen-pound bear trap; two Ballard rifles and two thousand cartridges; axes, hatchets, augers, draw-knife, hammer, saw, plane, a chest of small tools for repairing traps and guns, a change of clothes, a good supply of blankets, a stock of provision, consisting of flour, oat-meal, corn-meal, hard-tack, West India molasses, sugar, salt, tea, coffee, condensed-milk, and a few cans of "extract of beef," together with a large box of various small articles, indispensable in a camp-kit.

We felt sure we had got together enough to last us until the river opened in the spring, with the addition of the meat our rifles were to bring us. For we had planned a winter's campaign against the animals in the unknown country north of Parmachenee Lake (which is situated in the northwestern part of Maine) and the head waters of the Magalloway River proper. That northern wilderness was not known except to wild animals; for the most resolute hunters and trappers had never gone more than a few miles north of Parmachenee Lake.

A few sportsmen had visited the Lake, and a lumbering company had at one time cut logs near it, and drove them down the river; they had also built a dam a mile below the Lake, and a small camp; with these exceptions, the country was in its primitive state.

We, however, had formed a plan for exploring the valley of the Upper Magalloway, and also for making the trip profitable, by capturing fur-bearing animals.

The Magalloway after leaving the Lake flows still and smooth for a mile; then suddenly it dashes itself into foam over coarse boulders and slate-stone ledges all along a distance of five miles; then it gradually stills down, grows deeper, and less current for another five miles; after that, for twenty-eight miles, it slowly and quietly wanders along zigzag, forming a narrow opening through the dense evergreen forest which covers the broad valley without a break, except where some hunter or trapper built his camp for the season in some sheltered spot where a spring or mountain brook joins the river.

At Aziscoos Falls the river tumbles over mighty granite ledges, and enters the beautiful valley two hundred feet below, where it unites with the Androscoggin River four miles from where we were waiting with our luggage for the steamer *Diamond,* which would take us ten miles up the Magalloway River, to a settlement where we could get a farmer to take us on to the head of Aziscoos Falls.

While we sat there waiting and talking over our future prospects, a man came, up to us, and, as he seated himself on the end of a log, he said: — "Well, Barker and Danforth, I understand you are going to spend the winter on the Upper Magalloway."

We told him that such was our intention if our grub held out.

"Well, boys, you will spend a winter you will never forget. You will see sights and hear noises you little dream of."

We ventured an opinion that our rifles would put a stop to some of the howling. But our new friend laughed.

"You talk brave, but during the thirty years I have spent in the woods, I tell you I have listened to screeches that would make you forget your shooting irons; but you young bloods must learn for yourselves; you will not take advice from the experienced. But there is one tiling I will warn you against — that is the axe, which is more dangerous than any wild beast you will meet, because if after you are imprisoned by snow you should chance to split your foot open, as I have seen young hunters do, you would never see your homes again. So, boys, remember this bit of advice; and when you are well fixed in your home camp, eat a beaver-tail for Bill Whittemore; and when you come out, come and see me."

Just then the steamer came round the bend, and soon we were busy putting our luggage aboard; and meantime we could hear the passengers saying: "Those are the two hunters who say they defy cold weather and hungry bears."

On our way up the river we were asked many questions, some wanting to know of what our stores consisted, others about our ability to use our rifles in case of danger, and still others what we knew about trapping, etc., etc.

At Bean's Landing we put oar boats and kit into Lorenzo Linnell's farm-wagon, and he agreed to carry us to the head of Aziscoos Falls, eight miles farther up the river; but as it was getting late in the afternoon, we stopped with him that night. By taking an early start, the next day at ten o'clock we were at the end of public and private conveyance.

We settled with Mr. Linnell, and he immediately left us, and we were alone.

We at once launched, and when our luggage was all in, we found we had all both boats could possibly carry. We paddled up the river as far as the Narrows, a distance of ten miles, and the river as smooth and quiet as a mill-pond.

These Narrows are a sort of a sluice-way formed by two ledges which close the channel so much that the water rushes through with such velocity that oars cannot force a boat through during the high water of spring and fall; but with a tow-rope with which we fortunately had provided ourselves, we found no trouble in pulling our boats up, one at a time.

But it was now near night, and we camped just above the quick water. We left our stores in the boats, and for quarters pitched our shelter tent, made a bed of boughs, cut a large dry spruce which stood near, for firewood, cooked supper, and then as we lay under our shelter by the bright camp-fire we talked about our friends at home, and of what Whittemore had said about the northern wilderness and the axe, and came to the conclusion that wild animals could not scare us, and that we would cut wood, not our feet. The night, though in early October, was so cold that we were obliged to replenish our fire several times; and in the morning we found ice along the shore of the river, and the air was so sharp that we were glad to put on our mittens for a while.

At two o'clock in the afternoon we reached swift water, one mile below the foot of Parmachenee Falls, which is the point where the Little Magalloway empties into the main stream.

This swift water must either be poled up, or a man must wade it and tow his boat, because the banks are so thickly covered with alders and red willows that u tow-rope cannot be used ashore. We tried the pole, but found our boats were too heavily loaded to be taken up in that way; so we fastened the small one to the shore, and both took the other, and a long, hard, troublesome tug we had before it was fastened to the shore above. Then we went back for the other, which, being lighter, gave us much less trouble.

When we got the last boat up we went on shore, emptied the ice-cold water out of our boots, and wrung it out of our socks. Then a brief half-mile pull above the Rapids brought us to the junction of the Little Magalloway and the mainstream. Here the banks are low and covered with alders and willows, woven together with wild hops, und occasionally a huge elm pierces the tangle. In the centre of what seems a widening in the stream, is a huge mound,, rising to a considerable height above the water, and covered with spruce and fir trees. This sheltery green spot we chose as a safe place to laud our stores and to keep them from the animals which are usually annoying to a trapper.

We at once set about unloading our boats, and by the time our shelter tent was up it was dark. On the upper end of the mound we found driftwood for a fire. The night was far colder than the preceding one, but we piled on the blankets and slept warm. The next morning we went to work on our depot. We piled all the stores in as small a space as possible, then covered them with our shelter tent, and placed logs high around the sides.

At three o'clock in the afternoon, we took our knapsacks, filled with staple articles of food and two pail's of blankets, and followed the lumbermen's path across the country to the old logging camp, which we knew must be near the dam — about a mile below the Lake.

We found it somewhat out of repair, but we at once agreed to fix it up, and use it as our home shanty; but all we could do that night was to clean out the old cook stove which the lumbermen had left, gather boughs for our bed, and cut wood for the night fire.

Having thus set up "a home," at daylight the next morning we started back across the carry to bring our small boat; but we found it a job, for although the boat was light, in many places the trees were so thick that we were obliged to cut our road step by step. At four o'clock we had got it to the dam, and into the river above. Then we went on to the camp, and made a thorough clearing out of the old rubbish; but there were holes in the wall and part of the door was gone, and we could not fix farther without the tools; so the next morning one of us, in company with a rifle, went after them, to return at dark and throw down at the door a very large bear skin, but absolutely refusing to tell how he got it until "after supper."

After supper, however, it transpired that, stepping into the boat, to cross over to the evergreen mound where the stores were, he heard boxes tumbling about, and paddled across us fast as possible. His thought was that some one had followed us up river to steal our supplied. He landed in haste, and ran to the top of the mound, when, to his surprise, he saw a large bear swimming off for shore. He had got the scent and left. At once fire was opened on him. Of course he sank, and it took some time to fish him up, and more to skin him. He had not damaged our provisions much; but if we had not wanted the tools, and gone for them, he would have driven us out of the woods.

We at once decided that our stores must be moved to some safer place. Accordingly the next morning we loaded the boats and carried every thing a little distance up the Little Magalloway, to a very high bank, where we built a stout log fence around them and covered them with the boat. But this was a long, slow, hard job, and night was upon us before it was finished, so that we were obliged to build a fire and stay by it till morning. We had a jolly supper, however, of hard-tack and broiled bear meat.

The next morning we rolled the carcass of the bear under the roots of a big down pine, set our big trap by it, filled our knapsacks with traps, then crossed the carry to the Home Camp. By dark we had the door repaired, some of the largest holes stopped, and fresh boughs picked for the bed.

This old logging camp was twelve by sixteen feet, made of very large spruce logs, calked between with moss; the roof was of pine splits, well covered with spruce bark, and, after our repairs, it was comfortable enough, and with plenty of room to dry our furs and to keep a good supply of stores.

The next thing was to *get* the furs to dry. The first ones must be muskrat because after it freezes it is hard to get them. So the next morning after stretching our bear skin between two trees — by cutting holes four or five inches apart around the edge, and tying in strings, then tying the strings to the trees, making the affair look like a big spider's web — we took fifty traps, our rifles, and an axe, loaded them in the little boat, and started for the marsh at the head of the Lake, five miles from Camp Home.

Chapter Two - Setting Traps

THE marsh at the head of Parmachenee Lake is made up of crooked channels winding among small islands, and of floating mats which are firm enough to allow a man to walk on them, and all covered with a long, soft grass, through which the musk-rats have innumerable roads. Here we set our traps. Near the north end of the marsh, where a brook came in, we found a family of beaver. We soon concluded that they were engaged in building, as there was a house partially finished. We had no beaver traps with us, so we could not set for this valuable game.

We went back then toward camp, keeping close to shore, to see if we could find any signs of game,

On the east side of the Lake, about half way from the outlet to the marsh, is a long point made by the wash of a mountain-brook, which is called Moose Brook; around the mouth of it low bushes, about four feet high, grow so thick it is almost impossible to push through.

As we were paddling by that point, we heard sounds as of animals forcing themselves through those bushes, and we ran our boat under the overhanging willows that grew at the water's edge, and, rifles in hand, waited to see what they were.

In a few minutes two immense bucks walked out, threw up their heads, and took a look at the Lake; then they walked along a few steps, until they were not more than thirty feet from us; so close that we dare not move or even whisper for fear we should startle them. And then they saw us. We knew it was now or never; one bound and they would be back in the bushes out of sight. At the same instant we both fired. One deer dropped in his tracks, the other bounded over the bushes and was gone. We found we had both fired at the same one; but we were well pleased with our success, as it was a fine buck with six prongs on each horn. We took him along in the boat and went on to camp. We wished that we knew how to set up the head, but as we did not, and had nothing with which to preserve it, we cut out the piece of the skull' which would keep the horns together, and suspended the trophy up against our mossy walls. The meat we hung on trees near by, and the skin we kept to sleep on.

The next morning we went back to the Little Magalloway after more traps. Nothing had troubled our supplies, nor been near the carcass of the bear. After we got back to camp, we went on a tour of inspection among our musk-rat traps. We found thirty-eight fine fellows, took them out, re-set the traps, and went back to camp well pleased. It was nearly midnight before we had the thirty-eight skins off and stretched ready for drying.

In the morning we took four beaver-traps and went to the head of the marsh where we had seen the signs of beavers. We examined their works and, as nearly as we could judge by the teeth-marks on the newly-cut wood, there were eight in the family. A short distance up the brook there was a dam, and over it, near the centre, was a sluice, where they took their wood down; but the houses were built on a level with the marsh, and where the water was about five feet deep. In front of each house was a large quantity of white birch wood, piled from the bottom nearly to the top of the water, and so laid that it could be taken, a stick at a time, without disturbing the rest.

This wood was their winter's supply of food. They could come from the house, take a stick, carry it back, eat the bark from it, then shove the stick out into the open water of the marsh and let it drift away.

Some distance above the dam we found a birch eighteen inches in diameter, which they were evidently at work upon. They had felled it, and were cutting off the limbs to take to their homes. While doing this work they live upon the bark on the trunk of the tree, which is, of course, too large for them to move.

From this tree to the water — a distance of some twenty yards — a road had been made, and every root, bush, or overhanging bough, was cut so that their loads would not catch as they drew them along. Just where this road went into the water we set one of our traps, and fastened it by wedging a long pole into the ring of the chain, and tying the other end of the pole to a tree. (These poles are called "lolly poles" by trappers.)

The works of the intelligent beaver are examined very carefully by the trapper, not only to enable him to set his traps to the best advantage, but because by their works he can tell to a certainty whether the winter is going to be a long, cold one, with deep snows, or whether it is going to be an open one with little snow and the streams occasionally opened by rain-storms. If the winter is to be long and cold, the beavers work hard and lay in a large supply of wood; but if it is to be a mild one, they build their houses farther out of the water, and lay in very little wood, as they can get it fresh from the stump at almost any time. When getting their wood, they cut several trees partially off, and leave them for the wind to blow down; there were several of these selected and partially severed trees in sight around the pond, and to the ones they intended to take next their roads were made; and at the end of two of these roads we set traps, fastening them in the same manner as the first one.

In following up the Upper Magulloway from the Lake you find as pretty a river as man could ask to see: high mossy banks, about thirty yards apart, with pebbly bottom, and the water about two feet deep for the first two miles; then you come to a big eddy into which the water comes rattling over a rough bed from Little Boy's Falls, twenty rods above, which is formed by irregular shaped granite ledges, making a drop in the water of four feet, and forming a natural home for trout. The bank on the east side of the Falls is not more than eight or nine feet high, while on the west a sharp ridge runs along eighty or ninety feet in height, not only forming the bank of the river on one side, but also the shore of a pond about half a mile long, and nearly round, on the other side; and beyond this pond about fifty yards, is another one of about the same size.

The distance from the south end of the first pond to the marsh where the beaver were is short, so we carried our boat over and paddled around it. We saw some signs of game, but thought we would not set any traps until we could go about on ice. We then carried our boat across to the next pond, paddled round that, and landed at the outlet, which is at the end of the ridge, twenty rods below Little Boy's Falls. Four or five rods from the river, the outlet of the pond is about four feet wide, and after going about half that distance, the water loses itself among the gravel, and is seen no more; the bed for the rest of the way is dry.

When we neared the outlet we noticed a bad smell, and thought it probably a dead deer or moose. But on landing and looking around we found, where the water runs in among the rocks, a large quantity of fish, the most of them more or less decayed, but some yet alive. There were trout weighing from one-fourth pound to three pounds, but the greater part of the fish was suckers and dace; evidently these fish had tried to leave the over-stocked waters of the pond, and got caught in that natural fish-trap.

We took such trout as were alive — a matter of twenty-five or thirty pounds — to carry along to camp. While we were picking them up, we noticed that some of the fish were partially eaten, which caused us to look about more closely; and at last, on the opposite side of the stream where a big pine log laid, running back from the water, we saw a path. We crossed over, and found it to be a mink's road. It led straight from the fish to a hole among some big rocks a couple of rods from the stream. We had no small trap along, so we set the beaver trap in the road.

We returned to the Lake by way of the river, and went around to our musk-rat traps. We found the second night's catch not so large; there were but twenty-two. Taking them along, we returned to camp.

The weather which had been fine for a long time, now began to change; the sky was overcast, and the sun went down without any red in the west, and we knew a storm was at hand. As our supply of bread-stuff was getting low, the next morning at daylight we took our knapsacks, and bounced for the Little Magalloway. It had not stormed any, but we expected every minute that it would. We arrived at our depot of supplies in about an hour, very warm. We loaded our pack, then thought we would take a look at our big trap if we did get wet; and to our joy, we found in it a very large fisher. We reset the trap and skinned our game; but the storm did not wait for all this; it came in all its power, as far as quantity was concerned, and in less than fifteen minutes we both were wet to the skin, and we made tracks for the home camp as fast as possible. We arrived about noon, and after building a fire we gave the afternoon to drying our clothes, for we had not brought over any changes.

For the next two days we tended our musk-rat traps, and got wet, and dried ourselves, which was any thing but *fun;* yet we were as anxious to go to those traps every morning as though we expected to catch a bag of gold in them.

On the third morning we woke to find the rain had ceased, the wind blowing from the north, and so cold that we had to put on our mittens while crossing the Lake! We went to our musk-rat traps, then on to the beaver settlement. As soon as we came in sight of it, we knew that we had got one of the family, or had had one and lost him — which is often the case, because if the trap is not set so as to take him by the hind foot, the captive will perform a surgical operation and leave the trapper only a foot for his share; then he will alarm the settlement, and the inhabitants will invariably sacrifice their work and leave for parts unknown. While on the other hand, if the trap holds its victim, the beavers will only stop work for a while, and live on the supply they have on hand, and after a few days of quiet will venture out again, only to get their ranks thinned, and so on until the whole family have been taken one by one.

We knew at once that there had not been a beaver out for at least two nights, and there was no more wood drawn in than when we were there before. With eager eyes we hurried along to the traps; but before we reached the spot, we could see signs of a struggle; and sure enough there had been one in. On examining the teeth marks, where the captive had cut all that came in his way, taking the trap off with him, we found he must have been a big fellow and, doubtless, king of the ranch.

We looked for the trap, but could not find it. Next we looked for the pole, and with sorrowful eyes beheld only a part of that. The beaver had, as it seemed, after cutting every thing else, cut the pole, too, taking about two feet of it along with the trap. We decided at once to trace him.

So we very carefully examined along both shores of the little pond, and on the dam, over which they sluiced their wood, and we were on the point of going to look around their houses — a thing we did not want to do, as that would surely drive them away, if they had not already gone — when we espied the end of the pole downstream a short distance. We went there and found pole, trap and prize. He evidently had tried to go ashore to rest, and the chain had caught on a snag, and he had drowned. We took him out, and set the trap back where it had been at first. Then, taking the beaver which was nearly as much as one of us could carry, we put it in the boat and returned to camp. It was eleven o'clock when we arrived, and after a hasty lunch we went to the Little Magalloway and brought more traps, some provisions, and a change of clothes.

We did not reach camp until after dark. It had been growing cold all day, and by the time we arrived it was decidedly uncomfortable. In the evening we skinned our beaver; and to skin a beaver is no small job. The skin is slit from the end of the lower jaw to the root of the tail, then flayed to the legs, cutting the skin just above the feet; then the rest of the skin must be removed, when every part must be cut with a sharp knife — for it is so closely attached to a thick coat of fat that it cannot be pulled off like the skin of the musk-rat, mink or sable, and it requires the greatest care not to cut the skin. We stretched it by taking a long, slim alder, bending it like a hoop, and tying the ends together, then sewing the skin to it by passing a sail-needle, threaded with a long string, through the edges of the skin and around the hoop, until it was drawn as tight as a drumhead and as round as a dollar.

The next morning it was still cold, but we put on more clothing, loaded some traps, our rifles and axe, and our dinners, into the boat, paddled up the river, following the west shore of the Lake toward the marsh.

Chapter Three – Capturing a Caribou

MAKING up from the shore of the Lake on the west is a range of mountains, and with the exception of one point about half way up the Lake, the shore is bold and rocky. This point where it leaves the high land is narrow; then it widens out for some distance, then narrows again, and runs out obliquely toward the northeast, where it forms a deep cove, at the end of which is a floating island. This island rises and falls with the water; and around and under it trout gather in great numbers, and the otter, which live among the drift-wood and rocks of the shore, bring their young there to learn to fish.

We landed at the point near its widest part, and walked back toward the mountains. We soon found a well-worn path running from the Lake on one side to the cove on the other, and upon close examination we concluded that it was made by otter. We very carefully inserted a trap in the path at a part where it went over a log.

Returning to our boat, we went on toward the marsh; when we reached it, we were surprised to see the numbers of black ducks that had gathered there; and we paddled along under the cover of some overhanging bushes, until we were within range, when we both fired. We got one duck only, but more than five hundred rose and went off toward the south. We found but a few rats in the traps; we concluded that we were getting them thinned off, so we changed some of the traps to different localities.

We next looked at the beaver traps; but we found that they had not ventured out again, and we did not even make sure whether they were there or not.

We went back to the Lake, and followed the river to Little Boy's Falls, setting traps whenever we saw signs of musk-rat, mink, or otter.

On one of the ledges at the Falls we built a fire, broiled a slice of pork, and ate our dinner; then went on to the natural fish-trap. The rain had raised the water in the brook, and evidently some five or six hundred fish had tried to make their escape since we were there, and a large number of them were still alive. We took a supply for camp, and we thought we also could use some for bait, so we loaded our boat from the pile. We found a mink in the trap by the log, and we changed the large one for a smaller one, then started toward camp. Near the inlet of the Lake on the east bank of the river, was a big pine stump about five feet high, and hollow; into this we dumped our boatload of fish, then went on to camp.

It was now nearly the last of October, and we felt obliged to get enough of our supplies over to camp to last until we could use snowshoes and a sled. That was a hard job, to take forty or fifty pounds on our backs, and walk four miles with it; but we had it to do, so we went at it, making two trips a day until we had what we calculated would last us two months. On one of the trips we found a mink in the big trap, caught by the head; and nearly every trip we shot two or three partridges, which we carried to camp and tied up outside, to freeze them for future use.

The weather continued to grow cold, and on the first day of November we took up all our musk-rat traps. We had a good deal of trouble, too, in getting some of them, on account of the ice. And on that day we also visited the beaver works, and learned that they had not left; for we found one in one of the traps which we had set in their road to a tree they had partially cut down. The day was extremely cold; ice formed rapidly; places where we broke through on going into the marsh, were closed on our return, and it was very late before we reached camp.

On our way down the Lake we called at the otter's road and found one in our trap. He was alive and fought like a hero, but we at last dispatched him. In the evening we skinned him by cutting the skin from each hind foot to the root of the tail, and then turning it over the head, leaving the skin like a bag. We stretched it with three pieces of wood, each five feet long: two of them were one inch thick at one edge and one-fourth of an inch at the other; the third stick was one inch thick and shaped like a wedge; this we drove between the others with an axe. There is not much danger of tearing an otter skin, as it is very thick and strong.

The next morning the air was piercing, being the first time that the mercury had gone down to zero. We felt the cold more on account of the sudden change, as most of the time since our leaving the settlement the weather had been fine. We did not go out much, as there was work enough to be done in camp. We had a beaver and several musk-rats to skin and stretch, our clothes needed some mending, and these things busied us nearly all day.

We knew boating was at an end for the season; and that we must turn our attention to the hills and mountains until the ice was safe to travel on.

We had decided to set a line of sable traps up the Black Cat Brook Valley. This stream rises in the mountains to the east, and after flowing for eight or ten miles through several swamps, tumbles over coarse boulders into a deep ravine, and joins the Magalloway just above the old dam. It was up this brook we started one clear, cold morning with one rifle, an axe, some traps, and a bag of musk-rat carcasses for bait. We did not "blaze" as we went along, using the brook as a guide instead; but wherever we set a trap we "blazed" a tree, to mark the spot.

We set the sable trap by building an inclosure out of pieces of rotten logs, with a small opening on one side, in which we placed the trap, putting the bait in the back side and covering the whole affair with boughs after fastening the trap to a tree. We set traps along wherever we saw a good chance, until we reached the first swamp, where, in the centre, the sluggish brook creeps along, and on each bank for a space from three to five yards wide, the flat grass grows; then rises a strip of almost impenetrable alders which are joined by tall, straight swamp spruces where the green moss is ankle deep, and the dry, silky moss hangs almost to the ground, waving in the breeze as though to attract the attention of the caribou.

While we were standing there deciding which side of the brook to go up, we heard a tremendous splashing in the stream above. We dropped every thing but the rifle and axe and crept along back of the alders in the spruce growth for several rods. But soon the splashing ceased. We listened, holding our breaths, but could hear nothing. Then we crept along several rods further, and all at once we heard a bush break near the alders. We now laid flat down upon the moss, and hardly breathed. Soon we heard a step, then another and another, then the bushes began to move. One of us was lying on his side, rifle cocked and ready; the other lying in the same way, a few feet distant, and nearer the alders, with the axe. In an instant more the head and shoulders of a bull caribou came out of the alders not more than ten feet from us.

He instantly saw us. He gave a low bellow, and swung to go back the way he came; but in doing it, he got tangled in the alders. At the same instant we were on our feet. One of us shouted, "Don't shoot! let's catch him!" at the same time springing toward him; and before the caribou could extricate himself he was on him, but not much ahead of the other. Then alders, cariboa and hunters mingled. The struggle did not last long. We soon had him foul, with an alder bent down across his neck, one of us bearing down on the end of it. But we had acted without thinking. We had the caribou, but we could not keep him alive. In the first place, we had nothing to tie him with; and in the next place we could not get him to camp without a good deal of trouble. So after talking it over for a while we decided to end the performance with the rifle. He was a fine specimen, the horns measuring twenty-two inches in length, with nine prongs on one and eight on the other. Until after we dispatched him, we had not given a thought to our personal hurts. On examination we found our clothes nearly torn off, and scratches and bruises without number.

The power and strength of a caribou are astonishing. We could not have held him for a minute if it had not been for the network of alders which entangled his legs. He would have carried us through the woods at a rate that would have dashed our brains out against the trees.

We dressed off the caribou, hung the meat on high limbs of the trees, then built a small inclosure out of rotten logs, where we threw all the refuse, and also the head, after knocking off the horns. Then in a hole left in the side of the inclosure, we set a trap, covered it over with boughs, and laid big logs oh the top, so that no animal could get at the bait without going over the trap. The next thing we did was to build a rousing fire; and on the embers we broiled the tenderloin of the caribou, and, with the accompaniment of some cold bread, we called it a first-class dinner. We occupied the afternoon with trap-setting; and when night caused our return to camp, we took along some of the caribou meat and the horns.

Chapter Four - Making A Road to the North

It had clouded up during the afternoon of our caribou fight, and the. sun had gone down pale and cold. The next morning we resolved to try the ice on the river. To our great satisfaction, we found it would bear us. We went to the Lake on it, but found that was not entirely frozen over. While we stood looking off across the Lake, we saw on the tops of the big mountains a thick haze, and soon scattering snow-flakes appeared around us. They came faster and faster, until the air was filled with them. We returned to camp feeling as though the door of our winter prison was now being closed; and in fact it was. All communication between us and the outside world was to be closed for five months. The realization of this caused us to feel somewhat gloomy for a while, as we sat in camp thinking of home and friends. Were we to abandon the enterprise, and at the last moment pack up a supply of provisions and hurry out by way of the ice before the snow fell to such depth that we could not travel on it? When this question finally arose, it was instantly answered. No! We would not leave the woods as long as we were in good health and prospering in other respects. We would not give people a chance to say that we did not dare get snowed in."

But another and greater reason was, that we had formed a determination to explore the Upper Magalloway and at the same time to make the plan profitable. We were convinced that we could do it. We at once turned all our energies in that direction. First we must have snow-shoes and sleds. For nearly two weeks we worked on them, only stopping to look at the traps that were nearest to camp. The sun seldom shone, and when it did, it was through air filled with frost. Our snow-shoe bows we made out of yellow ash, hewing the wood into proper dimensions, then placing them in a trough, and pouring boiling water on them, and while they were warm, bending them around a form and drying them by the fire. After they were dry, we put in the heel and toe bars, which are pieces of wood going crosswise to keep the filling from drawing the bows together. Then we filled them with our caribou and deer skins, shaving the hair off with a sharp knife, then cutting them in strings, lacing them in after the Indian fashion, which is a very nice and particular piece of work.

Our sleds we made of silver birch, as that is tough and springy; the runners we cut seven feet long, and three inches wide, so that the sled would go over the snow without sinking into it much. The runners we placed fourteen inches apart, with posts three inches high, held together with thin slats, on which the load was to be laid. We made the sleds thus, that, narrow, they might run well in the path made by the snow-shoes.

These snow-shoes and sleds, which seem so little to build, occupied us, with our limited amount of tools, nearly two weeks, and we labored busily, too, often working late at night by the light of our beaver-oil lamp, which we contrived by putting a small roll of cotton cloth in a dish of oil, the roll being held in an upright position by means of a wire, the end about an inch above the oil; it had to be looked at often, for should the wick burn down it would set the entire lot on fire.

At last we got every thing completed, and ready for a cruise we tried our snow-shoes, and found them all right. But the snow was too soft, so that we could go only a very few miles in a day, and we found that little very hard work. The return to camp was easier, as we had the path we had made in going out. There were two feet of snow, and it lay on the ground as light as feathers; and we knew in all probability that there would be no change to benefit us until the January thaw. We came to the conclusion that the best thing for us to do was to begin making a road to the north, although we had no definite point for which to steer, and to run it northward eight or ten miles, then establish another camp, which would shelter us and our supplies while we should explore in its -vicinity. We thought best to keep back from the Lake to avoid the wind, as we must travel over our road almost every day to keep it trodden sufficiently hard for drawing our loads over when we felt ready to move what we might need of our camp kit.

We set about our road-making at once, travelling a little farther each day and "blazing" the trees, so that no deep snow should make us lose all our work by covering up all traces of it. We also set sable and fisher traps along the way, and each time we went over the road we drew along a piece of meat, so that the animals would follow the scent to the traps. This work tended to make our road-making much more agreeable, as we caught a sable nearly every day, and occasionally a fisher.

The weather continued cold, and snow incessantly fell, but not in the form the people two hundred miles south of us were accustomed to see; there the snow is heavy. This first snow was as light as feathers, and six inches of it would press down under the snow-shoes to not more than an inch in depth.

We kept at our task, and at the end of a week we believed we had a road five miles long. It passed over one high hill, where we saw signs of moose, then wound down through a rough country where the growth was all evergreen trees. Although we had not been able to get a view, on account of the falling snow, we knew we must be nearing some water course; it might be the river, or it might be a tributary; whatever it was, we were anxious to see it.

The morning of December 3rd., with our sleds carefully loaded with blankets, fry-pans, kettles, flour, pork, molasses, tea, sugar, salt, and a large piece of caribou meat, together with our rifles, axes, an auger, traps of different sizes, a good supply of ammunition, and a small box containing matches, gun oil, patches, needles, thread, extra mittens and stockings, we started from camp, determined to rough it until we decided where to locate; then to build a small camp. We knew it would be a cold job, but could last only a few days; then we would have comfortable quarters again.

It was 18° below zero when we started our sleds, but by the time we had gone a mile we were sufficiently warm, you may rest assured. Our loads went slow, and it was late in the afternoon when we reached the end of our road, where we built a fire and ate our dinner.

Then we tried to go on, taking our sleds with us; but as soon as we got into the untrodden snow, our sleds sunk so deep that we could not move them. The day was so nearly gone that we had to turn our attention to preparing for the night. We chose a thicket, sheltered from the wind by a bluff, where we shoveled the snow away with our snow-shoes, then built a small camp with three sides of poles covered with boughs; then shoveled the snow back against it, and with a fire in front, made of big logs, we put in the night, taking turns in sleeping and keeping the fire. We did not suffer with the cold, nor were we uncomfortable with the heat. In camping out at that season of the year, people are apt to be ready to move as soon as they can see to travel; it was so with us the next morning. But we did not take our sleds; all we took was one rifle, an axe, and some broiled caribou meat which we carried in our pockets.

We pushed on with our road-making as fast as we could, taking turns in going ahead. We covered quite a distance in the forenoon, owing to the descending ground, and a desire to locate a camp; still when it came time to retain, in order to cut wood for the night, we had seen no stream, nor signs of one. So another night we were obliged to take turns before the fire; but it was more comfortable than the first night, as the fire burned more steadily, because there was no snow or ice under it, to make steam to dampen it.

We did not oversleep, and were on the move again at daylight. It did not take us long to go over the track of the day before. Then again began the wallowing. It did not last long, however, as we soon came to the edge of what seemed an endless swamp, since the falling frost hid from view any trees or mountains on the opposite side.

We started to go out on the opening, but were obliged to retreat on account of water. We turned to our left, which we knew must lead us *down* stream if it *was* a stream, and a short distance took us where we could hear the water roar. We kept on in the direction of it, and soon we beheld with joy the largest beaver dam we had ever seen. We did not stop long to admire it, for we knew after we got a camp built to live in, we could attend to the fellows that built that.

We did not want a camp very near the dam, so we went down the stream some distance, where a spruce bluff made up from the stream, and the growth of timber was large. There we at once commenced operations. We worked with energy, but when it was time to go back to our shelter all we had accomplished was to get the ground cleared of underbrush and snow.

That night as we sat around our camp fire, and thought of the great beaver dam, we felt as though we had struck a mine; and indeed we had, if we were successful with our traps.

Before it was light the next morning, we had every thing packed on the sleds, and were picking our way amongst the trees, following our road.

The first thing we did on arriving at the chosen spot, was to build a bough-camp, like the one we had just left, to live in until we could build a log one. We constructed our log camp by laying one log above another, notched together at the corners, and then covering the structure with logs split open and hollowed out like a spout; the under ones laying hollow side up, and the upper ones hollow side down, with the edge of one in the centre of the other, then calking the under side: this makes a very tight, warm roof for a camp.

But this camp was not built in one day, nor yet in two. It took us nearly a week to get it comfortable and warm. In the meantime we had put some beaver traps at work on the dam, and they had performed their duties well, for we had three beaver to thaw out and skin as soon as we moved into our camp. We had not spent time to do this at the time they were caught; we could only hang them to a tree to freeze, so they should not spoil.

It seemed good to get inside of a camp at night and sit before a cheerful fire, after sleeping in a bough-camp for more than a week, where the wind whistled through, filling our faces with snow every time we moved them from under the blankets, the mercury down to zero and often lower.

But oar hard work was not yet done, for our provisions were low, and the road had to be trodden to keep it passable. So with nothing but an axe and the beaver skins on our sleds, we started for the home camp; and on our way we got several sable out of the traps that were set along the road.

Chapter Five - Under the Ice After Beaver

WHEN we reached the home camp, we found upon examination that we had not much provision there. But we concluded to take it all, excepting one day's rations, and go back and set what traps we could, then to return and make a road to our main supplies and draw them all over.

The next morning we loaded our provisions and a lot of traps, and again started north, taking turns drawing the sled. We spent nearly the whole day removing the snow from our traps along the road and re-baiting them; so that all we did after getting to Camp Zero (that was what we named our new camp) was to look at the traps on the beaver dam. We found we had made a misset; for in the trap which we had set in the main sluice of the dam, we found the forefoot of a beaver. This changed our ideas in regard to the best mode of handling the family of beaver. Our plan had been to go on the ice to the houses, cut holes, and set our traps near the entrances; but with the lame one to warn them, they probably would leave as soon as they heard us chopping the ice.

In the morning we decided to explore the swamp as thoroughly as we could before we set a trap. We found the swamp had been made entirely by the beavers. In a flat valley where once the banks of the stream had been about five feet high, the beaver had built their dam sufficiently high to flood these banks and cause the water to flow over into the low bushes on each side. So the way seemed open for us to experiment a little at the expense of the beavers.

In the first place we went to the north end of the swamp, where the brook was shoal and not very wide, and cat away the ice. Then we drove stakes close enough to stop the beaver, yet not to stop the water. Then we set a row of beaver traps along this fortification. By that time it was night, and we postponed work until morning, when we went to the dam with our axes, rifles, and three of our large traps, and commenced cutting away the dam. It was not long before the water began to settle in the pond.

Soon we heard a commotion far up the pond under the ice. To our joy the ice behaved as we planned, it being frozen hard enough to hang suspended on the banks and bushes. We kept steadily cutting, and the pond gradually grew less. Soon the water began to be mixed with sticks and mud; and all at once, not more than two feet from us, a huge beaver stuck his head out of the water, with a look of disgust on his face, which instantly changed as an axe, like a flash, dropped between his eyes, and in another minute he lay in the snow on the bank. Two more soon made their appearance and were served like the first one; the fourth came to the surface, out of our reach, and disappeared, to be seen no more in that locality. No more came after that; he had told the story. We cut the dam all away, so that where was once a pond there was now a valley roofed with an immense sheet of ice.

We then took our rifles and commenced to explore the wonderful works of the beaver. The walking was a little soft, but we didn't mind that. We never had had such an opportunity before, and we thought we wouldn't let it slip.

By following along the edge of the little brook which ran through the works, we could walk upright. And truly it was a wonder to survey the amount of labor which had been done by these industrious animals.

We found three houses and an immense quantity of wood piled at the entrance of each, all white birch. At each house as we came to it, one of us would discharge his rifle in the entrance and the other stand ready to shoot should any beaver run out; but we found no traces of them, and knew they must have gone up stream.

We saw musk-rats skulking along under the banks, but we concluded not to stop for them.

We kept along through the works and came out just below where the stakes were driven at a point where an eddy of the brook had worn the ice so that it had fallen when the water left it.

In our traps by the stakes we had four more beaver, one of them being the one we had robbed of his foot on the dam; the unfortunate fellow had put another foot in, and was at last fast. These were all alive, and made the shoal water boil with their big paddles. We soon quieted them with a club, and then hurried to camp to make a fire and change our wet, cold stockings.

We felt elated over our good fortune. We did not know whether we had captured them all or not, but seven were more than we had expected. After warming thoroughly, we brought our game to camp. Nor did we sleep until we got them all skinned, though it took us nearly all night. The skins we rolled in a pile outside the camp, that they might lie frozen until we could take them to the home camp for stretching.

The weather had been changing for two days, the sky was nearly clear, the few remaining clouds slowly going to the southeast, and when the sun rose the next morning after the slaughter of the beaver, it shone out clear and bright.

The hills and mountains that now appeared seemed strange to us, for we had been living in a perpetual snow-storm, where we could not see a quarter of a mile; and to have those mountains rise up before us all at once, was rather bewildering.

Across the brook, in front of our camp, was a high spruce bluff, and thither we went in hopes of a comprehensive view; but the snow-covered trees hid nearly every thing. So we chose a tall spruce which stood near a small one. This small one we climbed, and from the top of that scrambled over into the branches of the large one, then went to the top of it, where we sat with our compass until we had the mountains all well located in our minds, so that we should recognize them from any point. Then we turned our attention to the valleys. We could trace the Upper Magalloway from the Lake, which was plainly visible, to a point far up among the big mountains to the north. In some places we could see the river itself as it passed round a hill; then again only a sag in the trees betrayed its presence. Nearly northwest from where we were a high mountain towered far above everything else, whose sides were ledgy and covered with ice; and along the east side of this mountain the river seemed also to run.

We came down from our high seat and crossed to the river; where we struck it we found it was rapid. We tried the ice and found it both solid and easy to walk on; the intensely cold night had caused the river to freeze up, while the sun had thawed it sufficiently to flow over the snow; then a freezing period had followed; in this way the snow became packed and solid, and furnished the good travelling we found. We took off our snow-shoes and walked up quite a distance, but as we had not brought any lunch, we were obliged to return early.

Chapter Six - More Caribou

AT daylight the next morning we took our rifles and dinners and started for a tramp, a long one, provided the good travelling held out We found it about the same for a long distance, with now and then an open place where we could see the rushing water as it passed under the ice. The day' was fine; not a cloud to be seen. When we had travelled, as nearly as we could judge, on the ice for five miles, we came to what seemed to us to be smooth water, the river widening considerably. When we walked on to it, we found next to the ice, under the snow, several inches of water, so that we were obliged to put our snow-shoes on, which held us up dryshod. We had not gone far when we came upon tracks leading in all directions over the ice. We examined them and found they were caribou tracks, and very fresh. We walked along more carefully "for some distance, to a point from whence we could look around a bend, and see for a great distance up a straight stretch of the river. About half-way up this stretch we discovered an opening in the trees which stood thick along the bank. We went on quietly to this opening, and found that it was a pond nearly a mile long, and also what pleased us more, a drove of caribou quietly idling away their time in the sun. Some of them were walking round, some standing still, others lying down; we counted twelve in all.

We concluded to announce our presence at once, by sending two forty-four rifle-balls among them. They were, as near as we could judge, a quarter of a mile away; so we raised the sights on our rifles, dropped on one knee, and. after choosing our game, so not to make Another mistake and both shoot at the same one, we counted one, two, three, and pulled. Really it was a surprise to ten of them; but they could not fell where the sound came from, for the hills echoed it back from all sides, while we, after putting in another cartridge, kept perfectly still.

The caribou scattered in all directions, making tremendous leaps, then slowed down, trotting first in one direction, then in another, with their noses stuck straight out, their heads swinging from side to side, trying to catch the scent of whatever had caused the noise. Soon they turned toward the centre of the pond, as if they feared to enter the woods, not knowing where the danger was. Then we thought it time to try for them again; but at that instant they turned toward the two which lay on the ice, which brought them nearer to us; so we held our fire.

They cautiously walked up to their dead comrades. Some of the larger ones stood and looked at them; others trotted around them, sometimes going nearly to the shore. When we saw the big fellows remaining still near to the fallen ones> we did not let a chance slip; again counting one, two, three, the hills caught up the sharp crack and passed it back from bluff to bluff, and they seemed to centre it, and send it off down the valley with a dull roar, until it was lost in the distance.

Again the caribou performed in about the same way, only they had become more wild, and now moved in wider circles; but the air was so still that they could not get scent. We, with rifles loaded, waited for the next lull, which soon came.

The caribou returned to the point where the four were lying. They seemed to turn all their attention to one which was not dead, and was now struggling to get on his feet, but hadn't strength to do it. When we saw them quiet again, we counted as before and fired; one caribou tumbled as though knocked on the head with an axe. Another went down, but was as soon on his feet again, then down again, continuing this and all the while going toward the shore nearly opposite us, and giving utterance to fearful, groan-like noises. After working in that way for several minutes he seemed to gain strength, so that he seldom fell, and went for the woods with considerable speed, while the remaining number went round and round the sufferer.

It was plain that they meant to leave, and that we must take a flying shot, if any; so, raising our sights to one hundred and fifty rods, we aimed as best we could and fired. One more of their number was doomed to stay behind; but which of us did it we never could tell. We both claimed it, and had abundant proof to show *how* we knew who killed it. By this time the surface of the pond showed altogether a different look than it did when we first looked round the bushy corner where we had been concealed.

We went on to the spot where the caribou lay scattered on the ice, and viewed our stock of meat, thinking we were pretty "solid on the meat question" and also how much some people would like those handsome heads, which were of so little use to us. The first thing was to take care of our meat, which was no small job. We knew we should not have time to skin the animals, so we drew them ashore, dressed them and hung them up on poles placed against the trees. It was nearly night, but we determined to take a look for the wounded one that went into the woods. We could easily follow the track by the blood, but we did not have far to go, as his strength evidently had given out in trying to get over a fallen tree; and there we found him. We hung him up in the same manner as we had the others, then started for Camp Zero as fast as our tired legs would carry us.

The sky had looked hazy all the afternoon; and when it grew dark, no stars came out, and as we went picking our way down the river we were obliged to keep a very sharp lookout, in order to not fall into any of the open holes. We at last found the path that led from the river to the camp, and we had felt our way along among the trees nearly half the distance, when we were startled by a fearful crash, and a trembling of the ground, which we could not at first account for; but at last we concluded it was the hanging roof of ice over the empty beaver pond. The warm day had slackened the frost so that it could not sustain its own weight any longer.

It was midnight when we reached camp, tired and wet, as after dark we had been floundering about in the snow nearly half the time, and, the night being warm, it had melted upon us. We made a fire, got our supper, and had a chat about the Upper Magalloway, and wound up with a dispute about which of us had shot the last caribou.

Chapter Seven - Back to the Home Camp

THE next morning when we got outside (which was not very early) we found it was raining. This pleased us, for we knew that when it froze

— which would be in a few days at the longest — we could go anywhere we chose, as the snow would be settled down and packed hard; so we made ourselves at home in our snug little camp, feeling as though we ought to have a day of rest, although our provisions were growing short, excepting our supply of meat, on which alone we *could* live for a time.

All day the rain fell steadily; but before morning the wind came from the west, which changed the rain to snow; and this covered every thing with rough ice, making bad walking through the woods. On the river it was good, however.

So we availed ourselves of the opportunity to visit the traps round the river near the Lake, which we had not been able to do for a long time, and also to see a section of the river which we had not seen, which lay between Little Boy's Falls and Camp Zero. What the distance was we did not know.

We piled our beaver skins on the sled, and followed the brook on which we bad located the camp, to the river. Then down the river, which we found part of the way to be wide and still, at other places forming rapids between high banks; then through low alder ground until we reached the Falls. We judged the distance to be about three miles.

The first place of interest to us was the fish trap; accordingly we went directly there, where we did not find, as we expected, every thing frozen up. The stream from the pond up to the point where it ran into the ground was free from ice, and a few trout werc in it; thcy must have gone in after the rain storm, as they were not all dead; so we put some of the freshest on our sled, and left the rest for animals which, after all, had a better right to them than we had.

Tracks of otter, mink, and fisher, were plenty, and there was no knowing how many fish they had carried away. How the pond became stocked in the first place was a mystery to us, unless, indeed, the trout were natives of the water. Still we did not care very much, so long as it furnished food for ourselves and bait for our traps.

There was nothing in our mink trap by the log, but a road had been trodden hard in the snow that covered it. We dug it up and fixed it so that the unknown visitor would get caught the next time it tried to pass that way.

The fish lay too much scattered to set traps near, as animals could reach the food from any direction, and unless we placed traps on all sides we should not be sure of getting them; so we built a pen with three openings, gathered all the fish into it and covered it with boughs, intending when we came again to bring traps and set them at the three entrances.

Then with our sled we resumed our journey, crossing the ponds toward the marsh. The day was not very cold, but blustering, and for the last few hours the snow had been falling light and feathery as before the rain.

When we reached the marsh where the beavers were, we could see no signs of animal life; but with our axes we cut through the ice over the spots where we had left our traps, and we found beavers in two of them. They must have got in before it froze; still the cold weather had kept them in perfect condition. We could see no chance to reset the traps, so we took them along, together with the beavers.

When we got to the Lake we left our sled and went to the big pine stump into which we had put so many fish, to see if any animal had tried to get them. To our surprise and wonder we saw that the old stump had suffered terribly from the teeth and claws of animals, and were still more surprised as we approached to see the curious face of a lynx put up over the edge of the stump for an instant. Then with a bound that we had no idea any animal could make, the creature shot out of it, and the next instant was out of sight in the woods. We let two balls follow him; but either they were not sent in the right direction, or else they could not overtake him, for he got off unharmed.

The bark on the outside, and the rotten wood on the inside of the stump, were all torn off by the animals in clambering in and out. Through the sound part of the wood, which was about three inches thick, we cut two holes; and then going to our sled, we got two of our beaver traps and set them in these holes, as we were certain that the animals would go through them rather than over the top; still, to make the thing sure, we covered the top of the stump.

Then we went back to our sled, which now was not very light hauling, as it had for load seven beaver skins, two whole beavers, a trap, our axes and dinners; but we changed often about in drawing it.

We next went to a point about half a mile down the Lake, where we made a fire and ate dinner; while doing this, we saw a drove of caribou crossing the Lake near the outlet, about three miles away. We did not think of going after them, however, as we had all the meat we needed for a long time to come. After dinner we went to the floating island, then across the neck of land where our otter trap was. We dug the snow away, and found an otter badly eaten by mice and weasels; but we took it along, also the trap, as the snow prevented our setting it again.

Then we made for the outlet, which took us across the widest part of the Lake, where the wind and snow was all we could make way against. We saw the tracks of the caribou, but, none were in sight, the sharp wind having driven them into the woods. When we left the Lake our cheeks and ears were nearly frozen, but on the river, where the wind did not get such a rake, we soon got warm; and just at dusk we reached our home camp. It did seem good, indeed, to rest once more under its roof, amid the festoons of fur; for we had already a good display, of which we felt very proud.

We made our supper almost entirely out of venison, as we had so very little of our imported goods at camp.

Chapter Eight - Smoking Out a Fisher

THE next morning we commenced our task of getting provisions over the carry. The rain had not improved the snow-shoeing as we had expected it would, but had left it nearly as bad as it was before. The frozen part would almost hold us up, then all at once drop about a foot, which made our progress very slow and tiresome.

We did not reach our point of supply the first day, so it was fortunate for us that we ate mostly of meat the first night; if we had not, we should have been obliged to eat only meat the second.

The next day we got to the goods, and found them all safe; we went to the big trap, and found a fox in it nearly eaten by other animals; so much so that we did not take it. We set the trap again, and also took along some of the bear's meat, that on our way back to camp, we might set several traps beside our road.

The next day we staid at camp, taking care of our fur, stretching the beaver skins and skinning the otter and beaver which we got on our way from Camp Zero to the home camp.

For several days we drew supplies from the Little Magalloway, occasionally getting a sable; and one day we got a fisher, which gave us some trouble. He got into a small trap set for a sable, broke the chain that held it, and left; but the snow held his track, and we followed it. He went down the hill toward the river, where there is a craggy ledge in which he lived. We could see by the numerous tracks near a high crack where he went in, that more than one lived there. The crack was not wide enough for us to crawl in, so we commenced to smoke him out by collecting dry wood and piling it in the crack; then, with a lot of birch-bark, we set it on fire. At first it did not burn very well; but soon it took hold and roared up through the crack in the ledge as though a factory chimney was pulling it up. On looking up we saw what caused the strong draft; there was a hole in the top of the ledge some sixty feet above us.

We crammed the crack full of wood again; then with a good deal of trouble we climbed to the top. We found there a considerable surface, nearly flat, covered with trees, and one of them a very large pine. Near the smoke-hole we stationed ourselves with rifles, ready for any game, knowing no animal would go out over the flames through the lower hole. Just when we were at the point of giving up, thinking there must be some other way of escape for them, we heard sneezing and choking far down in the rock. Soon it was nearer. In another minute out jumped one fisher, closely followed by another: this one had the trap on his foot. We both fired at the first one, thinking we could get the other easy; but we found it a difficult job; any thing but easy.

The first one we shot dead about fifteen feet from the hole. But before we could put in a cartridge, the other went up a tree exactly as though he had no trap on him. The trap was light, find we thought it would stop him; but it did not, not even among the limbs of the tree. The tree was a spruce, and stood near a gigantic pine. From the top of the spruce he went into the pine like a squirrel. We both shot at him as he sprang about; but an instant more and he was out of sight in the snow-covered boughs near the top of the tree. We tried from all points to get sight of him, but could not. We thought of cutting down the tree; but this looked like a big job, as it was fully six feet in diameter. We knew we had not time to do it before dark, and before morning he would be gone; so with regret we were obliged to leave him. We had got one fisher out of the scrape, but we also had lost a trap.

We slid down the steep ledge and went back to the supply road where our sleds were, put the fisher on the load and went on to camp.

When we thought we had supplies enough over to last a month, we resolved to leave the remainder until after we should make another trip north, going still farther into the wilderness.

We thought best, however, before starting on this trip to go to the traps up the Black Cat Brook where we had caught the caribou, and to bring to camp some of the meat. When we reached the place we found the logs which surrounded the refuse scattered in all directions, and the trap gone. We travelled all round, looking for some trace of the animal that did it, but nowhere could we find any. The animal, whatever it was, had got into the inclosure before there was much snow; so we were obliged to give up the search.

From the traps up the brook we got two sable, then returned to camp loaded with meat, and made all preparations for an early start in the morning.

The next night found us once more at Camp Zero. We went by the woods-road, and found in our traps several sable, one fisher, and also a large horned owl, caught by one toe. The poor fellow was nearly dead. We offered him some of our caribou meat which we had left from dinner, and he ate ravenously. He did not seem in the least afraid of us. We took him out of the trap and tied him to the sled by one leg, then placed him on the top of the load. He tried to fly away when we started, but soon quieted down and rode to camp without making any farther objections. When we got there we took a light chain from one of the traps, fastened it to his leg with a thong, and chained him in one corner, where we fixed a pole for his perch. He made no trouble, nor tried to get loose, but sat on his pole with a solemn face, quietly studying our movements.

The camp seemed damp and cold when we first went in, but a good fire soon made it comfortable and home-like. In the night we were suddenly roused from sleep by hearing something walking around outside; soon after it was at the door; and then it commenced to gnaw. We took our rifles, and stationing ourselves one at each side the door, we pushed it wide open, expecting to see n panther spring in; but we found only a hedgehog, which we shot, and then returned to our bed of boughs.

The snow had been steadily increasing, but it was much better snowshoeing. Many of the logs and windfalls were so completely covered that we could walk over them without trouble. On the river the snow had settled the ice, so the water came up on it and froze, which made very good walking there, but not without snow-shoes.

Chapter Nine - The Fox without a Tail

OUR first trip was to be to Rump Pond, where we had made such slaughter among the caribou. Accordingly the next morning, with rifles, dinner, and hatchets, and with a few traps hung to our belts, we took the path from the camp to the river, which was nearly out of sight, being so covered with the snow which had fallen since we were on it; but with care we could follow it. Going up the river we saw where two otter had wallowed along through the snow for some distance between two open places in the river. We concluded that they were travellers, and therefore that it would be useless for us to set a trap for them.

When we neared the pond we walked cautiously to the place where we got so many lucky shots on the other trip, somewhat expecting to see another drove of caribou; but they were not there. But a fox was quietly trotting along just outside the bushes on the opposite side from us; so we stood still and let him come toward us. When he got within about one hundred yards we both cocked our rifles, put them to our shoulders and waited.

On he came, thinking of no harm, evidently, for he never raised his head, but trotted along as though he had a certain distance to make in a given time. About forty rods from us there was an angle in the shore of the pond which, when he passed it, if he continued on the pond, would bring him head toward us; so we agreed to shoot just before he reached that point. It was a small mark, travelling as he was, and at such a distance. But we liked long range; then if we killed we were proud of the shot, and often boasted of it afterwards.

At the signal we both fired. The fox went into the air, then twisted and tumbled in the snow, rearing sometimes, and falling on his back. We put in fresh cartridges, and thinking the fox was ours, walked leisurely toward it. When about half way to him he stopped his tumbling, sat up, looked at us for an instant, then with a leap that was almost a somersault, disappeared in the woods. We were greatly surprised, but we kept on, to see if we could discover the cause of antics so remarkable. We found that only one ball had hit him, and that one had cut his tail off. For there the tail lay upon the snow. We picked it up, and as we walked off in the direction of our meat another dispute arose, as we both claimed the shot that deprived the fox of his tail.

We found on reaching our meat that the animals were eating it badly, and that we must put it out of their way. But *how* we did not know, as it had been left in bad shape, and was frozen so hard that it was bad to handle. At first we thought of putting it all in a pile, and building a log pen to protect it; but that would require a great deal of work. Finally we decided to hang it so high that the animals could not get at it. But it required more strength than we had to raise one of them, for they were whole.

But we succeeded in doing it. By climbing a small tree we let our weight bring the top to the snow. Then cut it off at a point where it was about two inches in diameter, and passed this point through the gambrel of a caribou; then we placed a stiff pole with a fork on one end of it, under the bent tree, near the caribou, and raised it up until the caribou was several feet above the snow; and with the end of the pole firmly stuck in the snow, the heavy burden remained in position. We hung all the caribou in the same way, and then sat several traps around the refuse.

When this was all completed, we went to the one on the other side of the pond which ran off when we shot it. The animals had not molested it; and as we needed meat at camp, we thought best to take this one back with us. So we took our belts, put them through a hole which we cut in the under jaw, and used them to pull by. The caribou was frozen stiff, and it plowed through the snow on each side of the track made by our snowshoes. To overcome this difficulty, we knocked off the horns with our hatchets, turned it on its back, laid our rifles between its legs, and then one pulled on the belts while the other held it in position by taking hold of the hind legs as a man guides a plow. In this way we got it to camp without much trouble. We were obliged to put it inside to thaw, so that we could skin it. We stood it up on its hind legs, leaning it against the wall. About four o'clock the next morning we heard a dull sound, and almost at the same time our owl gave a tremendous hoot. We sprang out of bed, to find that the caribou had thawed so that his legs had given out, and he had fallen over into the fire. By the time we reached him the camp was full of smoke, strongly scented with hair. We had considerable trouble in getting the heavy weight out; and when we did, it was a curious-looking animal, and our camp needed ventilating.

We did not go to bed again, but began skinning the caribou by the light of our camp-fire, and this took us until daylight. The hide was so burned that it was good for nothing, and we threw it outside.

We cut the meat into pieces suitable for cooking, and buried it in the snow near the door. The tenderloin we broiled on the coals for breakfast, and after feeding our owl (which we had named Jared) we took our rifles, a few traps, and started to visit the fish-trap, and the old pine stump, to see if our friend, the lynx, had returned.

We found that no more fish had ran out of the pond, and that the mink and fisher were getting out of our log pen the fish we had put there; so we hopefully set traps in the openings.

In the trap under the big log we found a mink. After re-setting the trap we went along, following the river. In one of the traps in the stump was our lynx; he was still alive, but had been there too long to show much fight; we finished him with a rifle-ball. Taking him with us, we returned to camp by the same route, and in the evening we skinned the lynx and the mink.

Chapter Ten - Otter at Play

THE next morning at an early hour we were all ready for a trip up the river, to see the country beyond Rump Pond. We took on our sled blankets, axes, dishes, in fact every thing to make ourselves comfortable; and before starting we put a large piece of meat and a quantity of snow near Jared, so that he would not suffer while we were gone.

Our load was not heavy, and we could march along at a good jog, because the morning was cold, making us feel like moving briskly. When we reached Rump Pond we went to our meat, and with an axe cut from one of the caribou as much as we thought we should need. We did not stop for skin, but chopped the animal as we would a log.

In one of the traps near the meat was a sable, which we took out and tied to a tree, as we did not want to take it up river. After leaving Rump Pond we found the valley narrow and the river crooked. First a high bank on one side of the river, then on the other, covered with spruce and fir-trees, while the opposite bank would be low and covered with alders and scattering elms. At almost every high bank springs came out nearly on a level with the river; around these we had to step with care, as they were not' frozen over; and the river-ice in their vicinity was thin and treacherous.

But the beaver and otter were of a different mind, for around nearly every one of the springs they had played; and near one of them was a number of half-eaten fish which the otter had caught. After eating what they wanted, they had left the rest for owls and hawks, which are always hovering about on the water for such chances.

In some of the best spring-holes we set traps as we went along, to look to when we came back.

At noon we stopped on a high bank covered with spruce and fir-trees. There we made a fire and broiled some of our meat. After dinner we resumed our journey. The valley grew narrower and the river quicker, as we went farther up; and at four o'clock we reached a place where it was so rapid that it was not frozen hard enough to travel on. This put a stop to our further progress that day.

On the east side of the river was a thicket, where we concluded to spend the night. We built a bough-camp, cut a lot of fire-wood, and as the wind did not blow, we had a very comfortable night. In the morning we thought best to cruise round and not try to go farther with our sled. So with our rifles, and a good-sized piece of broiled caribou in our pockets. we started up river, going round the open and dangerous places.

Soon we saw that the valley was about to end in the northerly direction, for big mountains were just before us. Still the river must come through somewhere; so we pushed on to find the opening. We had not gone far when we came to a place where two streams of about the same size joined, one coming from the north, the other from the east.

The valley to the east was low, and the stream, as far as we could see, was covered on both sides with alders. But the one from the north came tumbling over coarse boulders, and its banks were covered with forest trees to the very water's edge.

We took this northern one, although we could not walk on the ice. But the woods were better than the thick alder bushes along the eastern stream. We had not ascended far when we heard the roar of water above the rattle caused by the current over the rough boulders.

When we reached the place whence proceeded the roar, a magnificent spectacle met our view.

On each side of a deep pool were ledges running upward in irregular shapes; and the water pouring in between them over a drop of several feet, caused the ice to form over them in fancy shapes. Down into that curious-shaped and glittering cistern the water disappeared with a dull roar.

Within this curious formation of ice two otter were at play. We stood and watched them for a while as they tumbled about like two kittens, but we could not resist the temptation to shoot; and at last we cocked our rifles, and with an understanding as to which should shoot the one on the right hand and which the one on the left, we waited until both heads were out of water, and then we both fired. We killed the pair, so that there was no chance for a dispute. We had some trouble in getting them, as we were afraid of the ice; but by means of a long pole with a noose on the end of it, we fished them out, and returned to camp feeling perfectly satisfied with our day's explorations.

We cut a large dry spruce into fire wood then rolled several of the logs on to the fire, and skinned the otter, rolled the skins in a pile, and put them on the snow to freeze. The next day we returned on our track to Otter Falls, as we named the icy spot, then followed the river up for, as we judged, about two miles. All the way it roared and tumbled over the coarse boulders, with occasionally a ledge; but we saw no more ledges like those at Otter Falls. The banks sloped down from the mountains on each side, and in some places it was so steep that we could not get along, and we were obliged to cross the river. This bothered and delayed us a good deal. Then, too, in some places large masses of snow and ice had slid from the mountains and completely dammed the stream. This water at last would cut a channel under the mass of snow, and the flood above would drain off. It was at these places that we made our crossings.

All along the river on the steep banks were deep, narrow paths running in all directions to spots where deer were yarding. Judging from the extent of the well-trodden paths, there must have been hundreds of them inhabiting the valley as far as we went. In the paths the tracks were very fresh, but we saw no deer; they all kept out of our way. We saw a good many sable tracks, but the other fur-bearing animals seemed to inhabit the lower valleys.

Soon after eating our dinners we retraced our steps, and reached camp just in season to cut our night's wood before dark.

Chapter Eleven - The Avalanche

Running parallel with, the river on the west was a high range of mountains whose bold sides showed huge perpendicular ledges, on which we could see large masses of ice hundreds of feet above us. And on the following day we attempted to reach the top of these peaks, in order to get a view of the valley through which came the stream from the east.

With a compass we got our course, then crossed the river; for some distance the land rose gradually, and the walking was good. Then for a mile we went up a steep slope; and it was all we could do to get up with our snow-shoes on. We had to cling to the trees, owing to the soft snow which would give way under us, causing us to fall headlong, filling our faces and necks full of snow. But a desire to got to the top forced us on until we reached the ledgy part of the range, which we at once saw was beyond our power to climb, at least, with snow-shoes on.

We followed along the foot of the ledge for some distance, trying to find some place where we could climb up. At last we saw one, and thought we would try it.

Taking off our snow-shoes, we stood them up against the ledge, with our rifles. We knew we should want both hands and feet to conquer the ascent. As soon as we were off our snowshoes we sank to our hips in the snow. To get along we were obliged to tread a path or crawl along on our stomachs: either way was slow work, to say nothing about its being hard. But we kept on. Sometimes a slip would send us back ten or fifteen feet headlong down the mountain, before we could catch at a bush or small tree; and often these were rotten and gave way, letting us down still farther, only the snow saving our heads from the rocks. Nearly every slip sent large masses of snow tumbling and sliding into the valley below.

In this way we worked for several hours, gaining a little, and at last we reached a gorge, into which the snow had slid from time to time, packing it, and thus making the walking a great deal better. Then we got along much faster. The gorge carried us up about half a mile, and then ended at a point where the ledge towered above us for more than a hundred feet, leaning out toward the valley, and looking as though it were liable at any moment to pitch over. On the edge of this ledge, directly over our heads, sheets of ice which must have weighed many thousand pounds, hung down. We felt, gazing upward, as though we had better make our stay short. We looked on both sides, but could sec no way to get above the perpendicular ledge. We then turned our attention to what we could see of the valley.

Seemingly just at our feet the crooked Magalloway, whose frozen surface looked like a white ribbon, found its way to Parraachenee Lake, which we could see many miles to the southward. At the foot of the mountain, not far from the river, two or three miles to the south of us, we could see three ponds, of which we made note, with the intention of visiting them. Our little bough camp we could plainly see, and a wreath of smoke curling up from the now dying fire that we had left in the morning. Just beyond our camp was a small pond, near the stream that came from the east. The stream for two miles above, where it joined the river, was swampy, with patches of alders interspersed with elms and water maples.

But beyond that hills piled on hills until the mighty backbone is formed which divides the waters of the United States and Canada. These hills were so piled together that it seemed as though there was no chance for a stream, and we could form no idea where the east branch came from.

We became so interested in this survey that we were not aware how the time was passing. But when we looked, we found it four o'clock. We did not take another look at the valley, but just let go our hold of the mountain, and down the gorge we went. At first it was sport until we attained a rate of speed that nearly took away the breath. Then we tried to stop, clutching at every thing in our way; but we had accumulated too much snow to control it easily, or at all; so we were carried on. We had only a few minutes to suffer, for the distance was not great enough to last long, travelling at such a rate. The snow was light, so the air was filled from the surface of the moving mass, and at times so thick that we could not see each other. We did not speak, but each tried with all his power to catch some bush, tree, or rock; all in vain.

Caught in the Avalanche

But just when we were on the point of giving up, for the snow had completely covered us, we experienced a curious sensation. We felt as though taken from the snow and passed along through the air very gently, and put down without a jar. For a few moments we were amazed, and stood wildly staring around, trying to look through what seemed to be a haze. All at once this haze cleared, and to our great surprise we found ourselves standing within five feet of each other, face to face, in the snow nearly to our shoulders, snug against a perpendicular rock about fifteen feet high. We looked at each other about a minute, before either spoke. Then we shook hands, and agreed that it was a good ride, but that we would take no more.

We had considerable trouble in getting out; but when we did, we took a look at the track we had left. We could see a straight track up the mountain as far as we could look, growing narrow as it went up.

The reason why we happened to drop so near the ledge was, that the snow was so light that as soon as we passed over the ledge, we, being heavier, *dropped through* the snow, while the bulk of it passed on over us. We were quite a distance born our snow-shoes and rifles; and when we attempted to reach them, we began to realize how tired we were. It required all our strength to crawl to them; but after getting our snow-shoes on, our spirits soon began to revive, and as it grew dark fast, we were stimulated to push on. It was quite dark when we reached our little bough-camp, and, fortunately for us, we had wood enough left from the two nights' supplies to keep us warm. Our supper *never* tasted better, and our bough-bed was as soft as feathers.

The next morning, after setting a few baited traps a short distance from camp, in different directions, baiting them with caribou meat, we took the sled with our otter skins and axes on it, and started down river. In one of the traps, in the spring holes, we had a beaver. We put it on the sled, reset the trap, and went along; in many places, the snow which was still falling had nearly obliterated the track we had made going up.

When we reached Rump Pond we went to the hanging caribou to get the sable we left there when we went up, and found another in the trap; we put them both on the sled, then kept on toward Camp Zero, eating our cold broiled meat as we went along.

On the river we saw where three caribou had crossed while we were gone.

When we were almost to camp, we heard Jared hooting; and as we went in he actually seemed glad to see us. He hopped off his perch and came as near as his chain would let him. He had eaten all his meat, so we gave him some more at once. After eating it he went back to his perch, and again assumed his usual solemnity.

It was nearly night, so we cut some fire-wood, built a fire, hung the sable and beaver near it, to thaw, so that we could skin them; but the otter we put outside. In the morning we skinned the sable and beaver, loaded all the skins on the sled along with our axes, and leaving plenty of meat and snow for Jared, started for the home camp, following the woods-road. We found one fisher in a trap on our way; reached camp about sundown, and found every thing safe.

For three days we stayed inside repairing our worn-out gear. Our snow-shoes wanted mending, our clothes were torn, our mittens and stockings worn full of holes. It was just the kind of work we needed, for the long tramps and the cold nights were beginning to wear on us, and we were in want of rest.

We wanted, too, to be in first-rate condition when the spring crust came, so that we could travel about wherever we. chose. And by the time that our clothes and snow-shoes were refitted, we both were again ready for the war-path.

Chapter Twelve - Jared

First we spent a day going to the Little Magalloway to look at the traps set along the carry; and as we had our sled we could, without any inconvenience, draw back a load. Out of the traps we got two sable, one nearly eaten by some animal; the snow covered the tracks so that we could not tell what creature it was. Our big trap we found so deeply buried that it would not spring. A lynx had walked over it and eaten a hole in the bear; we fixed it this time so that he would eat *that bear* no more.

We took some provisions and the rest of our traps with us to camp; then packed our sled with provisions for another trip.

The days were now be much longer that we could see quite a difference; and in many places, at noon, when the sun shone out bright, the snow would melt a little; still the thermometer each morning registered at zero, and often lower. And the morning of January 19th, as we left for Camp Zero, it was 14° below zero. We followed up the river, and crossed the Lake toward the inlet. The air moved slowly from the northwest, and we had all we could do to keep our faces from freezing by constantly rubbing them with our mittens. While we were on the Lake, and near the centre, we felt the ice tremble under us; and the next instant a loud report started from the northwest side of the Lake, and ran off in a south-easterly direction, sounding like thunder, but gradually growing less, until a distant rumble was all we could hear. Before the noise died away, the whole surface of the Lake seemed to move; and the shock was so great where we were, that it. nearly threw us down. But we were not standing riveted to the spot. We had abandoned our sled, and were going for the nearest land as fast as our legs would carry us.

We had not gone far when the noise ceased, and all again became quiet. We turned round, and could see the ice piled up in a line from the point where the report, started to the shore, where it had seemed to die away in a faint rumble.

One glance was enough to bring us back to a realizing sense of the situation, which made us feel that we had been foolish to get scared by a reef forming in the Lake which did not come within a mile of us. We had forgotten all about our cold faces; and we had no more trouble in keeping them warm the remainder of the distance across the Lake.

At the old pine stump we got a fisher, and found by the tracks around, it that there was another lynx getting his midnight supper there; so we replaced the trap for him to play with the next time he came there. At the fish-trap we got two mink and a fisher, then went on up the river, arriving at Camp Zero early in the afternoon. Jared again welcomed us with a hoot, and came to meet us as far as his chain would let him. His meat was frozen so hard he could not eat it, and the poor fellow was very hungry. After building a fire we thawed some meat for him; then we cut all the long feathers from his wings, so that he could not fly, and set him at liberty.

He was surprised when his wings refused to carry him. He spent nearly an hour in examining them, occasionally trying to make them perform their duty. After a time he gave it up and amused himself in the dark corners of our camp, peering into the holes and snapping his beak. It was quite laughable to see him come near us, as we lay on the bed, and look directly into one of our faces for a long time, as though studying every feature of it, then, without moving his body, turn his head so as to look in the opposite direction for nearly the same length of time at some other object.

As soon as it became dark he hopped around camp, giving utterance to the most fearful noises, ending each time with a prolonged hoot. We tried to still him, but all in vain. We were sorry we had cut his feathers off; if we had not, we would have sent him up the smoke-hole. We thought he would calm down after a while, but at midnight he was as wild as ever, and we could stand it no longer. So with a gentle toss, he found himself about forty feet from the camp, buried out of sight in the soft snow; he had passed over the fire and out up through the smoke-hole.

And now that every thing was quiet, we rolled ourselves in our blankets, hoping for rest and sleep; but thinking of the poor bird kept us awake some time. At last we began to lose ourselves, and in another minute we should have been happy, when that same unearthly noise, ending with a hoot, came in where the owl went out, and aroused us again. We thought we ought to bear the noise, as we brought the bird to camp and then cut off his feathers, so that he could not help himself. This loss of his feathers was what caused the lull in his noise when he took his departure from camp: he sank so deep in the snow he could not hoot, and it took him nearly an hour to get his head out; but the instant that it reached the surface, he had apprised us of it.

We laid back in our blankets and tried to forget the noise; tried to think of friends and the outside world; tried to see (in imagination) the Magalloway Valley as we saw it from the mountain; but all in vain. Every thing ended with a hoot. At last we got up, sat down by the fire, and talked it over, and came to the conclusion that it was our *duty* to shoot him; so one took a rifle, the other a birch-bark torch, and thus we marched out.

When the light of the torch fell on him, he never moved his head to see where it came from, for he was too busy finishing up the last half of a prolonged howl which was to end with a hoot. But the hoot that he was after never came; for his head was pierced by a ball. After this we slept. But before going to bed again we agreed never to try to tame an owl where the building was small and the nights cold.

Chapter Thirteen - The Big Snow Storm

IT now became necessary for us to have a camp up river; one in which we could live when the damp snow and rains in the spring should come. Therefore we decided to build it at once, and locate it near Otter Falls. So we took the tools from Camp Zero, and with what provisions we had loaded upon our sled, we started.

When we reached Rump Pond, we added to our stock nearly one-half of a caribou for up-river use. In our traps around the meat, we found three sables, which we tied to the limb of a tree, as we should have no time to skin them while camp-building. In our traps in the spring-holes we had an otter and a beaver; we left them as we did the sables.

For a camp location we chose a heavily-timbered knoll not far from Otter Falls, where there was a good spring running into the river. Our camp we built in the way we did Camp Zero; we also built a bough-camp to live in while building the other.

During the time we were building the camp, we were bothered by a snowstorm such as we had not before seen during the winter. It lasted two days and one night without cessation, making it almost impossible to go around even on snowshoes. This made camp-building very slow work, and before we got it completed our food consisted almost entirely of caribou meat. We were not able to explore any, and at the end of ten days we began a hasty march for Camp Zero. The first day we did not take our sled, as we knew we could not get through in one day. We only went to Rump Pond, where we got some more meat, and then returned to our new camp, not reaching it until after dark.

The next morning we took our sled with us, and as we went along we put the beaver, otter, and sables on it. A short distance below the Pond we left the river, and went into woods a little way, where we made a fire to cook our meat, for we had nothing but meat to eat. While we were busy broiling our meat, we saw the fire settle; but we thought nothing of it, as it often did so as the snow melted under it. But this time, when our meat was about half done, and the broiler was resting on two of the sticks which formed part or the fire, the whole apparatus suddenly disappeared. For an instant all was quiet. Then a volume of sparks and ashes came up from below and settled in all directions around us. Then all was quiet again. We looked down the hole, and saw at a glance what had caused the trouble. The place we had chosen for our fire was over a small mountain-brook, which had from time to time been dammed up by the ice, thus making quite a pond. This pond frozen over was the point where we had built our fire. After a time the water had worked away from under the ice, and the great fall of snow had made it look exactly like the country around it. Our fire had melted a hole through the ice, and gone down about eight feet.

We could see the broiler among the cinders, so we enlarged the hole with an axe, then cut a long pole, put it down the hole, and then slid down on it to the bottom, threw out the broiler, then climbed the pole. The meat was hardly palatable, so we tried another cut over another fire, which did not leave us.

Just at dark we reached Camp Zero, tired boys.

The next day we stayed in camp, living on caribou meat; but we rather do that than to try tramping, as we were very lame, owing to the heavy snow-shoeing. We thawed out the beaver, otter, and sable, so that we could skin them.

The next morning we made another struggle to reach flour and oatmeal. The day was a great deal warmer than any we had had for a long time, so that by noon we were nearly wet through. We went by the woods road, as we thought it would be easier; because there is no travelling so tiresome for a woodsman who is used to logs and holes, as a dead level like a lake or river.

By the middle of the afternoon we saw we could not make the distance, for we were getting very leg-weary; with every step our snow-shoes sunk about two feet, to be raised only to sink again. So we left the sled and returned to Camp Zero, rather than lay all night by a fire in the snow. The next night we reached our home camp, and never had we supposed that bread *could* be made to *taste so good* as the bread we ate that night.

It had been nearly two hundred hours that we had lived entirely on caribou meat, and nearly all our food had been meat for several days previous. It seemed to us we never should want any more caribou; and our work had been such that we wanted and needed a larger amount of food than usual.

We had taken several sable on our two days' tramp from Camp Zero, and also got very wet, for the weather continued warm, and when we reached our home camp, the sky was overcast and looked like rain. We sincerely hoped it would rain hard for twenty-four hours, for that would make the snowshoeing better. We were determined not to go on any more long tramps while such travelling lasted; and, fortunately for us, there was a change. The 'second morning when we looked outside, the rain had arrived; but large snowflakes were also falling. The thermometer registered at thirty-six degrees above zero; but unless it moderated still more, we knew the snow on the ground would not settle much; still, should it make a crust that would bear us, it was all we would ask.

By noon the snow ceased to fall, and the rain came in torrents; but about sunset the wind sprang up from the north, and our hopes were crushed. In a very few minutes the air was again full of snow, and we began to feel gloomy. There were five feet of snow already on the ground, and if one or two more came, we should be obliged to stay near camp all the time; at least, we could take no long tramps; and besides, our traps would be covered, and nothing caught, which, in reality, was the thing we cared about. We had already captured enough to pay us well for our venture; or rather we believed so. But we had no definite idea what our furs were worth; and often when we got a nice skin, one would say to the other:

"What do you think that is worth in Boston?"

Chapter Fourteen - Thirty-Five Degrees Below Zero

THE next morning the sky showed a still different aspect. The fast-flying clouds were scattering, and the air was very sharp. Our thermometer registered just at zero; two inches of snow had fallen in the night. We tried our snow-shoes, and found that the rain had improved the walking somewhat, but that it needed more frost to harden it.

We went to our traps up the Black Cat Brook, where we got one sable; but we found most of our traps were two feet under snow. As we had nothing else to do, we dug them out and re-set them.

The wind was blowing considerably, and we thought that the reason why we grew so cold, in spite of our extra exertions. As we neared the camp, we were obliged to run to keep £rom freezing. After building a fire and warming ourselves, we took a look at the thermometer; and to our great surprise it was 20° below zero I We thought it was not strange that we were cold. At night the wind went down; but all the evening we were obliged to keep the old stove red with heat, to make the camp at all comfortable. At ten o'clock we went to bed, but not to sleep. We did not dare to do that. We had always been comfortable in the camp before, therefore we knew it must be an awful night. We were afraid, too, that our wood would give out. Finally we rose and took some of our blankets and made a room just large enough to hold ourselves and the stove. Then, each taking a blanket, we put it over our shoulders like a shawl, and sat there almost astride the stove. By doing this, we used but little wood.

The night was a long one. More than once we thought of home and plastered walls. We had no fear of really freezing, for we could live a long time inside by cutting and using some of the timbers of the camp, as we could replace them when it grew warm again. But this we were not obliged to do.

As soon as it was light enough, we examined the thermometer, and found it 35° below zero. We remained in camp during the forenoon; until we had used up every available stick of wood. After dinner the question arose whether we should cut out the inside timbers of the camp, or go to the woods for more wood. It was finally decided that we should put on extra clothing and try the woods first. We could stay only long enough to cut a few sticks, then run with it to camp, where we would warm ourselves, then go again. In this way we got enough for another night.

When we closed the door for the second night, the thermometer stood the same as in the morning: 35° below zero. It was necessary that we should have some sleep, but we did not dare to both sleep at once. So with stools, and sticks of wood, roofed with boughs, which we took from our berth, or bed, we made a place for one near the stove; just in front of it. We then took turns sleeping and keeping fire. Thus we passed the second night; our wood more than lasted through, but we should be obliged to replenish during the day.

Early in the morning we looked to see if the cold wave had not passed, but the thermometer registered 33° below; on the rise, but so little that it did not help our case much. We waited until near noon, and found it had risen to 20° below; but we could feel no evidence of its being any warmer. We got our wood the same way as on the day before. Toward night the mercury went lower again; and when we closed the door for the night, it was back to 35°.

Another night we took turns in sleeping; but toward morning we could tell that there was a decided change; and when we looked out, the sky was overcast, and the thermometer registered 18° below zero. We were happy, and at once began to cut wood, resolved to always have in future at least one week's wood on hand.

By noon the thermometer told us it was zero weather again, which was as cold as we cared to see it at any time; but by dark it was a good deal warmer, and we made our bed in its old place, and slept soundly all night.

For two days we did nothing but cut wood and carry it to the camp, piling all we could inside, and the rest near the door just outside. We at last had what we thought would keep steady fire for ten days; and that would carry us through any cold snap we could expect. During the time, the air was full of falling frost, but no regular snow storm; and gradually the air cleared, so that by the third day it was nice winter weather again; about zero in the morning and 20° above at noon. Thus it stayed for several days, during which time we had reached our camp near Otter Falls. This camp we had named "Camp One," it being the first above Camp Zero, in the series we proposed to build.

We looked at all the traps on the way; out of them we got one otter, two beaver, and a sable; we took with us a number of traps, and nearly all the provisions we could draw. The first day we cut wood to provide against another cold snap; then we felt ready for explorations.

Chapter Fifteen - A Canal Dam

THE first trip was to the little pond we had seen back of our bough-camp, from that outlook on the side of Ledge Ridge. We found it only a short distance; something less than a mile; and inhabited by beaver. They had built a dam at the outlet, raising the pond so that it covered nearly twice the ground it originally occupied, making a pond fifty rods across. On the east side, quite a large stream came into it, and almost on a level with the pond.

Beside this stream we discovered quite a large spring where the water boiled up in many places, forming an opening in the ice about thirty feet across. Just back of the spring were three beaver houses.

The water in the spring was full of newly-peeled sticks, where the beaver had left them; and there were several roads made in the snow from the spring to the point they cut their wood; about six rods away.

We set four traps in the water where the roads commenced, securing them with poles fastened to stakes driven into the ground where the water was deepest. Then we went on following up the stream which ran along a bank about twenty feet high, while the opposite bank was not more than a foot high, and covered with alders as far as we could see. We found as we went up the stream, that it turned more into the north, and that the valley was growing narrow very fast. At all the holes in the ice, we saw traces of either otter or beaver; but finding no good spots to set traps, we kept on. After going about one and one-half miles, we discovered we had been following a *canal* instead of a mountain stream, as we supposed; for there was the main stream before us, where there was a dam about four feet high, pouring a part of the water into this canal, which turned off at a right angle, forming a narrow passage where the bank was about six feet high. This arrangement formed a perfect guard against high water in the pond where the beaver lived. It was indeed a wonderful piece of work, and showed that judgment was used in the planning and building of so extensive a work. We could hardly believe our own eyes, and walked all round it several times, to satisfy ourselves that it was not a "flood jam" that caused the water to cut through the bank. But we could see signs of beaver everywhere. The narrow sluice was evidently made by the beaver, for all the roots had their teeth-marks on them. We spent nearly two hours examining the work before we were satisfied to leave it.

Then we followed the main stream toward the river, going on the ice where it would holds us, and for the rest of the way pushing through the almost impenetrable alders.

We saw no more beaver or otter signs. But soon after we reached the river on the ice, not far from our camp we saw two caribou quietly feeding on the moss that hung to the limbs of a tumbled-down tree. They did not notice us until we were within fifty yards of them. Then they heard our snow-shoes, and for an instant, without raising their heads, seemed to listen until the}' located the sound. Then their heads came up, and what a surprised look they gave us! Evidently they had never seen such creatures before, and did not know whether to run or not. Meanwhile we were steadily walking on, and were within twenty-five yards of them. The air was perfectly still, and doubtless they could get no scent of us. It seemed all the time as though they intended to jump on us if we went near them. But all at once they gave a snort, and the next instant all we could see was a mass of flying snow as they disappeared around a bend in the river below. We could easily have shot both of them, but their skins were worthless, and we had all the meat we needed, so we let them run.

The next morning we followed the river up nearly to Otter Falls. Then we turned toward the east, skirting the alder ground, and struck the Branch some distance above the canal dam. There we found the water rapid; but the snow had become so deep that we could walk on one side or the other, crossing on bridges made of jams of ice. After travelling about a mile, we found the stream resembling the river above Otter Falls: steep banks on both sides, with game-signs scattering. There were plenty of deer, and we saw several caribou tracks; but these did not interest us much.

Near noon, where we ate our dinner, we found a stream coming in from the north. Up the valley it looked level; so we followed up that valley, and found all along signs of beaver. In some of the openings along the stream where they came out, we set traps; but night forced us to return before we found where they lived.

Early the next morning we were back there, and pushing on up the brook, where we found a swamp through which the brook ran, and a dam which covered it with water. Here the beaver lived; not far from the dam up the brook, were three very large beaver houses.

On the dam where the beaver went over, there was a low place where the water was swift, and it was not frozen; at that point we set a trap, then went back to high ground, and walked along the edge of the swamp for about half a mile, when we came in sight of a pond nearly a mile long and a fourth of a mile wide.

Beyond this pond the mountains rose to a great height, forming a deep basin in the centre. It was a wild, solitary looking place. The sides of the mountains looked to be thinly covered with trees, and the tops were one mass of snow and ice. We had only a few minutes for a survey, as we were a long distance from camp. And before we reached it, we found that we had stayed longer than we ought. Night overtook us long before we reached the river. It was with a great deal of trouble that we followed our snow-shoe track to camp.

It was very evident that if we went any farther in that direction, we must build another camp. But we decided to first explore the main stream. We started the next morning, following the river. We found good travelling. The big snowstorm had formed banks outside of the bushes and trees, on which we could walk past the open places while passing the rapids.

About three miles above Otter Falls the appearance of the country changed. Instead of the deep, narrow valley with steep sides, we found a wide, level country, over which we could look for miles. The river again became wide and still, with swamps frequently making back and several rods across. This made the river look very wide in places, as the five feet of snow had levelled all the bushes. Everywhere game-signs were plentiful. We went through several miles of the level country, then returned to camp fully decided that that was the valley in which to build our next camp.

Chapter Sixteen - Farther into the Wilderness

ACCORDINGLY, the next morning, with all our provisions, blankets, axes, and a large piece of caribou meat loaded on the sled, we started, not knowing just where to locate, but resolved to take the best place we could find.

Oar sled went along well in the track which we made the day before; but when we reached the end of that, a great deal more power was needed to pull it along; but we kept it along with us.

The country was nearly level for two miles beyond our track; then we reached rapid water again, where the mountains came almost to the stream. Where the rapids ended, the river was wider, doubtless a large eddy, but so covered with snow and ice that we could not make sure. On the east side of what we called the eddy, near the rapids, there was a small spring brook tumbling in over ice-covered rocks. Near that brook we chose our camp ground.

First we built a bough-camp to live in while building the log-camp. Then early and late we labored on that. It was a great deal of work to remove five feet of snow from a place large enough to build upon, with nothing but a snowshoe to shovel with. But the weather favored us. There was no storm during this time. If it had been a little warmer, it would have suited us better; but we did not complain. If our fingers stiffened with cold, we would go to the fire which we kept burning in front of the bough-camp, and warm them.

After completing our camp, which we named Camp Two, we set a number of traps not far from it at different points. Then leaving what provisions we had, except enough to last us to the home camp, and a good supply of wood, we started down river to look to the traps, and bring back more provisions. The first night we stopped at Camp Zero, although reaching it long after dark. In the morning we separated, one going over the hills by the woodsroad, the other down the river and across the Lake, arriving at the home camp before sunset. We looked on our furs which hung about the walls, and at those we brought with us, with a great deal of pleasure. We got on this trip two beaver, one otter, four mink, one fisher, and eight sable. We were nearly all the next day in skinning these, and when they were added to the rest, it was indeed a nice show. But we were not satisfied, and were sorry enough that the winter was so nearly gone; nothing but big snow storms, reefs forming in the Lake, or extreme cold weather could make us think of home. But busy as our minds were in thinking about fur, there was one other thing we had not forgotten, which waa to see with our own eyes where the Magalloway River came from. We had a vague idea that if we could reach the swamp, spring, or pond at its head, we could almost kill game with a club, as we had found it more plentiful and not so wild the farther north we went. Therefore we were bound to see it, or something unforeseen would happen to prevent us.

Upon examination we found we had scanty stores at camp for a long trip up river. So we went to the Little Magalloway for more. And we were greatly surprised to find how low our supplies were there. We had taken load after load away without looking to see what was left. We found we were running low on almost every thing, and just at a time when we needed these things most.

We decided to draw every thing to camp, then count the days we could stay and trap, and divide the provisions into that number of portions.

The next day we went two trips to the Little Magalloway, which took every thing we had. We also took along the big trap, together with all there were on the carry, to the camp, as we could not go to look at them, since we should be up river most of the time. Besides, the game was mostly caught along the line, although we got a lynx in our big trap when we went for our first load of supplies.

When our goods were all at camp we divided it; not in day rations, but weekly. We reckoned on nine weeks yet in the woods, so we divided it into nine equal parts. These parts looked small, but we agreed to fill the bill with caribou meat and partridges, of which we had seen hundreds, but had shot only a few. We had plenty of cartridges, so we could have a change in the meat. We put our allowance for two weeks on the sled, a number of traps, and two hundred cartridges.

At daylight next morning we started up river across the Lake. The weather was fine, sky clear, and no wind. The sound of our voices would echo among the hills as we talked of the sights and the game ahead.

That night we stopped at Camp Zero. We got there early, and put in our time cutting wood, to keep the supply good. At the fish trap on our way up, we got two mink, but nothing had troubled the old pine stump. The next day as we passed Rump Pond, we stopped and took on a big pile of caribou meat. That night we reached Camp One.

The next day we went to the traps up the branch, taking the sled with us, passing the canal pond where we had two beaver in traps set near the spring. We took them along to the dam on the branch at the head of the canal, and there we left them until we came back. Up the pond brook we got two more beaver. Along our way we were looking for partridges, and got six during the day; but they seemed more scarce now that we wanted them. From the canal dam the four beaver made nearly all the load that we could draw. Before we went to bed we skinned them, and that did not allow us much sleep that night.

The next night we were at Camp Two early enough to cut a good supply of wood, and to look to the traps in that vicinity before dark.

The next morning we started with our pockets well filled with caribou meat. We took no other food, determined to make our supplies last if possible. We had also some traps, our hatchets in our belts, rifles and a plenty of cartridges. We found the rapids were short, and above them that the ground to the northwest as far as we could see, was covered where there were any trees, with "bog-spruce."

To the north and east the mountains rose to hundreds of feet in height, and came close down to the river's bank. We followed along up the river, finding brooks coming in on all sides, and soon it was hard to tell which was the main stream, and finally we gave it up. In among the several branches were what looked like fields covered with snow. At first we thought they were ponds; but we soon saw that they were too uneven for that. Upon pushing down a pole, we found they were covered with a growth of moss. Then we knew that they were open bogs; that is, destitute of trees. They were crusted sufficiently to bear a man, except in some places where there was no snow. Those places were mud-holes where small springs came up to the surface, but did not discharge water enough to form a stream to carry off the black mud which lay in them like porridge. We pushed a long pole into one of them, but found no bottom. How deep the porridge-like mud was, we could not tell.

Chapter Seventeen - The Mired Moose

OUR attention was soon attracted to the many tracks of animals around one of these mud-holes. Upon going to it, we saw a curious sight. The mud-hole was about thirty feet across, and nearly round; the banks of snow, which were five feet high, made it look like a shallow well.

All around it near the edge, were claw marks where the fisher, the lynx, and even the sable, had slid in, then climbed out — if they were so fortunate as to work their way through the thick mud to the bank again — bringing with them a coating of mud which they had strewn over the snow for rods on all sides. We could see places where they had rolled and slid through the snow, evidently trying to rid themselves of the mud before it froze.

At first we could not see what induced the animals to risk their lives in that quagmire; but on close examination we discovered hair. Cutting some long poles in the nearest timber, we commenced to probe. At last we felt something hard, but it was too far from the edge for us to raise it to the surface, although it was not more than a foot below. Our curiosity was excited. We *must* know what it was.

While we were standing there, planning how we should raise it, we saw a lynx come boldly out of the woods and steer straight for the mud-hole. He never looked around, showing plainly that nothing troubled him. We cocked our rifles, and let him come until he was within seventy-five yards of us, when he stopped, looked round towards the woods where he came from, looking, as we thought, for his mate. But the chance was too good to be lost, so we both fired. The lynx rolled over dead; but we never forgot the sound those rifles created. On either side there was the sharp bark of the fox and the piercing screech of the lynx, and these sounds were taken up and repeated by the owls in the deep woods, startled by such an uproar — the deep woods where, in all probability, such a din was never heard before.

For a few minutes, fur was not what we were after. We were looking for the nearest and easiest tree to climb, and thinking of what Whittemore told us on the steamboat landing at Errol. But the yelping, screeching, and hooting gradually grew less and more distant; and it being *rather late* to explore the mud, we returned to camp, taking with us our lynx, which was a big one. Perhaps we should have returned immediately to camp if it had been earlier in the day; although both of us declared we were not in the least scared.

Early the next morning we took several traps, our axes and rifles, and started for the bog again; for we were determined to know what those animals were after in that mudhole. Before reaching the desired spot, we saw where several lynx, fisher, and foxes had crossed our trail, showing that they were uneasy, and were hunting for the cause of the noise the day before.

The first thing we did after reaching the mud-hole, was to cut from the nearest woods scrub spruces, draw them to the hole and throw them in, one upon another, until we had built a bridge that would bear us from the bank of snow to the object of our search.

Then we cut two long, strong levers, which we pushed under it, over the edge of our bridge. Then putting the weight of ourselves on the levers, we brought to the surface the remains of an immense bull moose, with a full set of horns, which showed he must have got mired there in October, or early in November. In all probability, fighting near there, be got pashed backward into the hole, and had been unable to extricate himself.

It was a bad mess to do any thing with; but we determined to profit by his misfortune. So we secured the ends of the levers by pushing a strong stick over the end of each into the hard snow which formed the banks. Then we set several traps on the bridge, knowing that when a snow storm came it would cover up all the tracks we had made, and that all the animals would travel along the bridge to reach the bait.

The raising of the moose and the setting of the traps had taken us nearly all day; so we returned to camp as soon as the job was done.

Chapter Eighteen - Lookout Mountain

WE now were obliged to turn our attention in another direction, and let the mud-hole remain quiet for a few days. Following up the river to the point where it divided into so many branches, we went up the north branch far into the mountains.

After going up for a short distance, we found it came tumbling down over the side of a mountain which changed from the evergreen trees to a scattering hard-wood growth. The mountain-ash was very plenty, some of them quite large, nearly a foot in diameter. Nearly every one of these ash-trees had been peeled by moose as high as they could reach. Their tracks could be seen in all directions, some old, some new. The snow was so deep that it had been hard work for them to get about, and they had peeled every thing that was in sight which they considered eatable.

We saw some signs of sable, but not enough to warrant us setting traps so far out of our way as that would be. So we returned to camp, getting there in season to cut more wood for the next cold snap. We got quite a number of partridges, to which we did ample justice at supper time. Caribou meat we considered a little dry.

The weather had been growing gradually pleasanter since the three cold days; the sun melted the snow in many places at noon, and this improved the snow-shoeing so that we could go through the woods very well, except on the north side of the mountains, where the snow was still soft, not getting any sun. As we did not care to trouble the animals on the open bogs until after a snow storm, so that they would not be shy, we decided to try mountain-climbing again. A little to the northeast of the open bog, nearest our camp, there was a mountain towering far above its - surrounding companions. This we chose for our lookout. But we well knew it would be impossible for us to reach the top in one day from camp; so, taking our blankets, axes, and three days' provisions on the sled, and our rifles in our hands, we started at an early hour.

After leaving the bog we relied entirely on our compass, which took us over hills and through deep valleys, often where we were obliged to turn to the right or left, and then help each other up some steep ledge, drawing the sled after us as best we could.

On all the spruce ridges the deer were very plenty, and on some steep places the snow was dug entirely off, where they had fed on the ground hemlock.

Occasionally we saw the signs of moose, but nowhere that of caribou. From the bog it looked like one mountain sloping down to the stream; but we found it very different from that. It was not until late in the afternoon that we began to climb the mountain. Then for a mile we went through open hard wood, where the walking was good, except that the grade was rather steep for snow-shoes. All through the hard wood moose-signs were plenty; peelings and browsings on every side; and we saw several places where quite a number of those huge creatures had laid down, forming deep holes the size and shape of their bodies.

Near night we stopped and built a boughcamp beside a spring which bubbled up and ran away down the mountain under the snow. It was a clear night; not very cold. The moon shone in among the snow-covered trees, the sparks from our campfire curled up, swinging this way and that, trying to find their way out through them, while we idly watched them as we lay on our boughs enjoying the heat of the fire and trying to realize bow far we were from human habitation, and that if any thing happened to us no one could lend us a helping hand. But we knew we were all right, so we let the gloomy side vanish, and enjoyed the winter scene before us. Soon our eyes grew heavy, and we slept the sleep of the hunters.

As soon as there was any light in the morning, we were all ready for a start. We did not take our sled: all we took was meat in our pockets, and rifles in our hands, intending to be back there at night. We pushed on as fast as we could, so as to reach the top of the mountain before the wind rose, should there be any.

We found the climbing harder as we neared the top; the ground rose faster and the trees grew shorter and nearer together. We went through moose-yards for awhile; then every thing seemed to have deserted the almost barren waste. The trees grew thicker and shorter, until it was almost impossible to pass among them; this lasted about half a mile. Then we reached the point above vegetation; and the top of the mountain looked like a big snowball, buried for half its bigness in the mountain. The walking was good, and we were soon at the top. The wind had not risen, and not a cloud was to be seen.

For the first few moments we gazed with wonder, turning from side to side, trying to take it all in at one glance, as though the scene might vanish and we lose the chance of examining each valley.

But the great panorama did not vanish. Nor could any thing drive us from the spot until we saw all, unless it was the cold, and we felt that we could stand that for some time amid such scenes.

The first thing was to determine by the compass which way was south, as we felt much interested in that direction. We found that it was directly down the mighty Magalloway Valley, where we could see innumerable ponds and bogs which, covered with snow as they were, all looked alike. We could only get glimpses here and there of the river; yet we could trace it among the hills the entire length of the valley. Parmachenee Lake we could not see, it being hidden from view by Ledge Ridge.

Toward the west, just at our feet, was Moose Bog, and farther on, the hills and mountains mingled together as far as the eye could reach. Farther on we noticed an opening cut through the woods resembling a road which seemed to climb for the largest mountains and highest peaks. We examined it for several minutes, trying to ascertain where it ended in the distance. As we lost sight of it in that direction, we looked nearer, and found that it ended where vegetation ceased — on the very mountain we were on. Then we looked to the east, and there we saw the same mighty line stretching away from mountain to mountain, until it was no larger than a thread.

Then we began to realize what it was!

It was the National Boundary; and we stood between the United States and Canada.

To the southeast of us the mountains were not so large, and seemed jumbled together without any regularity. From east to west, on the north side of the mountain, was nothing but an endless sea of mountains as far as the eye could reach, covered with an unbroken wilderness. We knew that the boundary was on the height of land that divided the waters of the St. Lawrence on the north and the Androscoggin on the south. Therefore we were beyond the head of the Magalloway; and as it was a part of our winter's operations to find out where that came from, we once more directed our eyes to the southwest, following out each stream separately as it ran to Moose Bog, which in reality was the long-sought-for head of the river.

On none of the streams could we see any ponds or bogs, although the mountainous country might hold many which were not visible.

Having satisfied ourselves that we knew now where the Magalloway came from, we left the top of the mountain, glad to exercise, for we were fast becoming numb.

Our trip back to the little bough-camp did not take more than half the time we had consumed in going up. We reached it early, and did not leave it until morning. We had time to cut plenty of wood, and the fire we had that night was large enough to roast an ox over. It made it so warm in the small camp that we slept without blankets. The next night we got back to Camp Two, where we talked over our trip late into the night.

Our provisions were not quite gone, but as there had been no snow to cover up our signs on Moose Bog, so that we could to advantage declare war with its inhabitants, we thought best to go to the home camp, look to all the traps, and bring back more rations. The travelling was good in our snow-shoe tracks, so we did not stop at Camp One, but kept along to Camp Zero; we did not reach it until after dark. We found we had a beaver in one of the spring-holes, and a sable at Rump Pond. We had shot a good many partridges, so we took fourteen on our sled with us, to leave at the home camp as a safeguard. But having nothing on our sled to take that night, except blankets, which we could carry in our hands, we left the sled on the ice where we crossed the brook, as we should go that way in the morning. It was about ten rods from camp.

When we went to it in the morning we found the partridge feathers covering the snow for rods around the sled. On counting our birds, we found only six. The thief had left tracks, so that we saw it was a lynx. We took two more of our partridges, tied them to a long pole, which we stuck into the snow at an angle of about forty-five degrees, letting the birds hang down to within about three feet of the snow.

We then put a beaver trap fastened to a heavy stick under it, and covered all with snow.

Then hauling our sled, we went to the home camp by the woods-road; we got three sable and a mink on our way. Our pile of fur was growing steadily, for we brought some with us every time we came.

About this time we began to worry about it some, thinking there might be some stray fellows roaming through the woods, now that it was better snow-shoeing, and if they should reach our camp soon after we left, a snow storm would cover up their tracks so that we could not trace them, and the pay for our hard work would be gone. But we could see no way to protect ourselves at present; but later we would take in our traps round Camps One and Two, and confine ourselves to the Lake and country round, where we could be at the home camp each night.

We were in hopes it would not snow until we got back, as we had rather wait a day for it than to draw our loads through it so far.

But the next day as we were crossing the Lake, it commenced and lasted until we reached Camp One, which was on the second night, then it cleared, and again the wind, as usual, began to put it in piles wherever it could get a hold. At Rump Pond, as before, we put a large piece of caribou meat on our sled, to help out the flour, oat-meal, and hard-tack, our corn-meal haying all disappeared. The lynx at Camp Zero had not been back. Evidently he had had enough to last him for quite a while; but we left the trap set, so that when he did come it would be a surprise when it took hold of him.

We stayed over a day at Camp One; and went to the beaver traps up the branch, and to the pond brook, where we got two beaver; and it was so far, and out of our course, that we took up all the traps down to the canal dam, leaving those in the little pond back of the bough-camp.

The next day we went to Camp Two, setting sable and fisher traps along wherever we thought there was a chance to get any game.

Chapter Nineteen - The Lynx Fight

THE following morning we were ready to visit the Moose Bog, and also to commence operations that would take some of the howls out of those animals which could not scare us. We took our sled: on it we put our axes, a good number of traps, also a rope which we brought from the home camp, and with our rifles, went directly to the mudhole where the moose was.

To our great satisfaction, we found that the animals were again at work on it, and with redoubled vigor. The traps we had set on the bridge were so covered with snow that they did not spring, which we were rather glad to see. The first thing we did was to fasten the rope to one hind leg of the moose. Then one of us stationed on the bank, pulled on the rope, while the other chopped off as much of the body, together with the leg, as both of us could draw up out of the hole. The flesh had frozen on account of our leaving it out of the mud as we had; but it had the odor that would attract an animal from the Rocky Mountains, if they liked moose meat.

We carried the section which we had drawn out of the hole across the bog to the edge of the woods, where we set a trap, hanging over it, on a limber pole, a piece of the meat. Then we drew our load a short distance farther on, where we set another trap, baiting it as before; and so we kept on all around the edge of the bog until our stock of meat was gone. Then we went back to the mudhole and repeated the operation until we had a line of traps entirely around the bog, also along the track where we drew the meat; so that wherever any animal struck the way to the bog, the scent would lead into a trap.

We had been so interested in our work that we did not think how time was passing; and we were obliged to hurry on our way back to camp. We left our sled on the river a short distance below the bog, as we confidently expected to have some game to draw back in the morning. And so it proved. For the next morning as we neared the bog, we could hear cursing, and even swearing. We knew the inhabitants were in trouble. So we quickened our steps, thinking we could be of some service. But upon arriving at the scene of action, there were so many involved we hardly knew which to help out first. Hesitating, and turning to look around, we saw two lynx in a quarrel, and thought that was the place for us to show our authority. As we drew near them, we saw how the quarrel had commenced.

One of them had been able to pull up the long stake which fastened the trap, and instead of going to the woods as he should have done, he went straight to his neighbor, as his tracks in the snow showed, probably to settle some old account.

They were so much interested in this matter that they did not mind us. We walked to within twenty feet of them and stopped, trying to make out which was going to get the case; but it was impossible to form an opinion. We could not tell one from the other. They were about equal in size and strength, and seemed to have claws all over them, except at one end, which was teeth and eyes. At least, if there were not claws all over them, there were marks of them. At times there was nothing to be seen but a mass of flying fur, and out of it came sounds resembling the tearing of heavy cotton cloth, when their teeth and claws tore through the skin and flesh.

It was impossible for us to put a ball into the revolving mass with any certainty; but we stood with rifles cocked, ready for the moment when they should be quiet. With hair nearly on end, we listened to the fearful screeches to which they were giving utterance, mingled with the tearing of flesh and clashing of jaws. It was several minutes, though it seemed an hour, before they gave us the opportunity. Then we put a stop to the fearful work. Their skins were so torn and bloody that we considered them worthless, and left them where they were, taking the traps away with us.

The report of our rifles had a different effect than at the first time we fired on the bog. Instead of the terrible uproar, silence almost instantly prevailed. Every animal seemed to try to hide himself. And it was not until we approached them, that they showed signs of struggling. Then they fought to the last. It was useless for them, for we soon had them all so that we could handle them.

Then we took our sled and went round the circle, loading on the animals, and also the traps, as we thought it best to let "well enough" satisfy as, and to go to the home camp, where we could guard our riches. We had, thanks to the unfortunate moose, taken in our traps during that night, five lynx, two of which we did not take, eight fisher, four sable, and one fox, which, together with our traps, made all the load our united strength could draw. But never did two trappers pull, prompted by more thorough satisfaction, than we did. We would not have changed places with the President of the United States.

The idea was, we were happy!

That night and the next day we were busy skinning the animals and hiding our traps, depositing them in a hole we had discovered in a ledge a short distance back of camp. Our object in putting them in a ledge was to guard against fire, so we should be sure to find them the next fall, for we had already planned another trip in the Upper Magalloway Valley.

Chapter Twenty - Gathering in the Traps

THE next morning we loaded all the things on the sled that we should want at the home camp, such as blankets, fry-pans, broiler, plates, cups, pail and axes; also what provisions we had, and our fur. After that was done and the sled drawn out upon the river, we took a farewell look at the deserted camp, and at the sign we had made and fastened over the door. This sign read:

All parties are welcome to the use of this camp and are requested to leave it in as good condition as they found it. Any one destroying it will incur the ill will of **Barker and Danforth.**

The day was fine and warm; the long cold winter seemed to have left its deep bed of snow for the spring to quietly send on to the Atlantic. A few birds crept from the deep woods, and were happy in the sun on the yet snow-covered banks of the river. Squirrels, that we had rarely seen during the winter, were also among the happy denizens of the forest.

The great accumulation of snow on the limbs of the trees began to let go its frozen hold, and in nearly every direction through the forest, we could hear the dull thud as it buried itself in the snow on the ground, and the trees seemed to sway to and fro, trying to balance themselves after getting rid of the heavy burdens which they had carried so long.

Every thing seemed to feel the change; and we shall never forget the day as we, with joyous hearts, took our loaded sled to Camp One, which was far above Zero, staying there over night. It did not take us long to gather in our traps, as they were not very far from camp; the farthest being those in the little pond back of the bough-camp, where we got a beaver, which we skinned near the place.

The next morning before leaving, we put a sign over the door, which read:

Welcome! Any one occupying this camp can return thanks to
Barker and Danforth.

We disposed of our traps in the same way as we had the first, lot, then followed the river toward Camp Zero, gathering the traps as we went along. When we reached Rump Pond our sled was so loaded that we stopped to hide our traps in a ledge on the east side of the river. Those traps which were around our caribou we let remain, as we should be obliged to make another trip to get the remainder of the meat, which was in good shape, owing to our having left the skins on. The hair had kept it from thawing during the bright sunny days.

By the time we reached Camp Zero, our load was all that we could draw along, as we were very tired.

Chapter Twenty-One - Who's Afraid of a Lynx?

THEN we got to the brook where the trap was left under the suspended partridges, we found it gone. The tracks, though dim, owing to the melting snow, we could see, and we were sure it was the lynx. But he was nowhere in sight. We drew our load to camp, then looked for the trap. The track of it we could only occasionally see in the snow; this showed that it was in the air most of the time. We looked for the stick which had been fastened to it, and found it just where we left it. It was frozen fast in the ice; evidently the first jump the lynx made had broken the chain, leaving nearly all of it attached to the stick.

It was so near night that we postponed our search until morning. We left all of our skins outside to freeze, and before starting on the trail in the morning, put them inside to keep them from the sun, so that they should not dry any until we got to the home camp, where we could stretch them.

The trap after leaving the partridges, evidently had gone straight for the thickest growth of scrub-trees in sight, which was about ten rods up the brook on the south side; at this point it seemed to have amused itself for quite a long time by knocking the bark off the trees and breaking small branches; then it had started along, getting behind every stick and upturned tree, thus causing itself and the lynx a great deal of delay until it reached higher ground, where the open growth had less attractions for it. At this point we began to understand its motive. There was a pile of huge granite boulders about half a mile beyond. There we expected to see the trail end at the entrance of some big hole. And we were right in our conclusions.

Sure enough, under one of those big stones the trail went. The hole was large enough for one of us to crawl into; but either we did not want to go, or through politeness one waited for the other. Finally we introduced a long ^ole, which was seized when it had been pushed in about eight feet, and we could hear fierce growls. Then we cut another pole, and cut off one limb, so as to make a hook, trimming all the others close. This we tried for a long time to hook into the trap; but at last we found our hook bitten off, and the end of the pole chewed to splinters. Then we tried a smoking-out process, similar to the way in which we smoked the fisher.

Our fire had hardly been lighted when we could hear the rattle of the trap, as though it was getting uneasy. Yet it did not come forth. We stood away from the mouth of the hole, not caring to meet the trap too unexpectedly. We looked on all sides, to see if any other hole would betray itself by sending forth smoke, but there was evidently no other.

Our fire burned low, and we replenished it with a good stock of pine wood from a dry stub which stood near. Instantly the flames more than filled the hole; they climbed up the rocks and licked the overhanging snow. The heat was so great that we had to step back in order not to burn our faces; and it was fortunate for us that we did; for at that instant our fire shot out of the hole as though a keg of powder had exploded behind it, and the lynx, with open mouth and glaring eyes, came too through the whirling embers, deprived of his side whiskers, and the tassels on his ears, which did not improve his looks in the least.

We both fired at him, but this did not stop his headlong career. The trap was an impediment, and caused him many a tumble, but did not delay him so that we could get a second shot before he was out of sight, under another rock.

It was hard medicine for the lynx, but we could not help laughing at the sight which must forever remain in memory. His long hair was all burned off, which made him look leaner than is usual with a lynx; and besides, the fire had taken all the fight out of him.

We had spoiled the skin, yet we wanted the trap; so we tried him the second time. The place where he had gone in was where several boulders about twenty feet in diameter, lay close together, forming, with the great amount of snow, deep, dark alleys, thus giving him a good lot of room to operate in. It was no use to try the smoking process here. We must contrive some other means to drive him out. The plan we adopted was to follow him into his ice-bound cave with birch-bark torches, and either shoot him in there or drive him forth.

The first thing was to gather the bark, which did not take long; then we rolled it into as close rolls as we could, then pushed it into the ends of split sticks. We made three of these torches, but it being inconvenient for the one which had the rifle to carry any thing else, we left one outside. Then with a light in one hand, and a fresh torch in the other, we began our search for the trap.

The passage was not wide enough for us to go side by side, nor high enough to walk upright. We were obliged to crawl along and keep as close together as we could. But we had little fear of the lynx giving us battle, for we thought he had got fire enough to give the torch a wide berth if he could.

After going in about twenty feet, we found the cave would not amount to much in summer, as the sides, and also the roof in many places, were clothing but snow and ice; and we also saw that deep holes ran back, made by fallen trees which held the snow from the ground, and that these would give the lynx plenty of chances to hide himself from us for a long time.

But we kept on, the torch giving light enough to see some distance ahead. We proceeded for some time without seeing any signs of him. The torch was nearly burned out, and we were obliged to light the other. Still we had not reached the end of the passage. We pushed along faster, to reach the end and return before this last torch should burn out. But we had not gone far when a cold feeling suddenly crept over us, and it was not owing to the damp atmosphere, but to the sound that reached our ears, the unearthly yells of the frightened lynx as he got sight of the torch. It is needless, perhaps, to say just how quick we reached the opening, where we instantly changed the torch for a rifle, and proceeded direct to camp. We were fully convinced that we did not want the trap. It was past noon when we got home, so we did not leave until the next morning; but before night we had taken up all the traps in that vicinity, and hidden them. If any one had been near us that afternoon, they would have heard this question asked many times: "Who's afraid of a lynx?"

Chapter Twenty-Two - Moving Caribou Meat to Camp

EARLY the next morning we started for the home camp. We left our blankets and camp kit, as we wanted to use them once more in Camp Zero.

The weather continued fine. The snow had melted so much that during the night it froze hard enough to allow us to walk over our road without snowshoes; but outside of the road we could do nothing.

So with our skins, axes, and snow-shoes on the sled, we marched along very easily. We took up all the traps by the road as we came to them, putting them on the load. About noon the sun had so melted the snow that we were obliged to put on snow-shoes again. In several places the deer and caribou had walked along the hard path, evidently to rest their legs, for wherever they left it they were obliged to wallow to their sides.

If deer had been what we were after, we could have killed dozens in a day, because it was now impossible for them to run. But our stock of caribou meat, which was far better, being killed early, and still in prime condition, was all that we could possibly consume before we left the country. When we got within about a mile of our home camp, we hid our traps in a big hollow birch tree, as there was no ledge near that we knew of, and our load was too heavy for the soft snow.

After leaving our traps we got along better, and reached our home camp a little before dark, where, to our relief, we found no one had been; and now, with one exception, we should be there every night until we started down river.

It may seem strange to some that two young fellows, born and reared in thrifty country villages, not known to each other until we had left the parental roofs and gone out into the world for ourselves, then meeting as by accident, and almost without knowing each other, should agree to trap a whole winter on the head waters of the Magallowny River, and should become so much attached that we were no longer acquaintances, but brothers, and at last should feel very sad to think we had but a month more to be together and in solitude. Yet such was the fact; and that evening we talked long about our future. We arrived at no definite conclusion, only that we would spend the next winter, too, on the head waters of the Magalloway.

We thought it best to get our meat from Rump Pond the first thing, and put it where we could keep it frozen. So, long before light the next morning, we were picking our way along toward Camp Zero with both sleds. Nothing had disturbed the old pine stump, but at the fish trap we had a mink. We did not take it with us, but left it until our return. We reached Rump Pond long before noon, and at once set to cutting all the good meat from the remaining caribou. This we packed on the sleds, storing the remaining traps with those on the ledge. We found our loads of meat all we could draw, so we did not take any of the horns. We did not care particularly for them, as our homes, for years to come, would be where our hats hung.

The snow got soft in the afternoon, which forced us to leave our loads some distance from Camp Zero, and go in for rest. But as soon as we could see the next morning, we were pulling on them again, and it did not require more than half the strength to move them over the frozen snow.

When we reached Camp Zero we put our blankets and camp kit on the sleds, and over the door we put a sign which read:

We leave this camp the 28th day of March 1877, *and will return the* 15th *day of October* 1877.

Barker and Danforth.

Then we hurried along with our loads before the snow should thaw. A little before noon we drew up to the door of our home camp. Toward night we scattered our meat so that no two pieces could touch, that it might freeze during the night. Afterward we buried it in the snow to keep it frozen.

Our stock of imported goods looked rather small, but we did not think of going for more, or of quitting the woods; but each day ate just as little of them as we could, living almost entirely on meat.

Chapter Twenty-Three - A Ride on a Buck

THE high range of mountains which runs down from the north on the west side of Parmachenee Lake, seems to stop to let a deep cove in beyond what should have been the shore were the Lake regular in its shape at the south end. Beyond this cove, a ridge some forty or fifty feet high stops the water from running on through a swamp to reach the Little Magalloway. A mile and a half beyond, where it widens out and runs through a flat country, it is known to a few as Long Pond; and whoever fished at Parmachenee Lake, usually spent a day at Long Pond, for it is alive with fish.

It was for that pond we started the next morning after we got our meat to camp. We took along a few traps, our hatchets and rifles. The morning was fine, and as we walked out upon the Lake from the river, the sun came over the mountains and shot his rays over ns into the head of the deep cove, spreading there a pale red light, and still farther on toward the west the ice-covered top of Bose Buck Mountain shone like sheets of silver.

The trees which had got nearly rid of their winter's load, looked gray. The birds seemed to increase in number each day, and while crossing the lake we saw the first migratory bird of the season — a crow.

The walking on the Lake was splendid; we carried our snow-shoes slung on our rifles until we got to the head of the cove. There we were obliged to put them on, for the snow in the woods where there was no track would not bear us without them.

Partridges were plenty, sunning themselves on the branches of the dead cedars which lay along the edge of the Lake partially buried in snow and ice. They would allow us to approach within thirty feet before they would fly. We did not shoot any, as we did not like them to eat, because their meat tasted too much of the buds on which they had lived so long. The few we shot up river had satisfied us on that point.

As soon as we entered the woods, we began to set traps wherever we saw a good and likely place for animals. We could not judge of this by the tracks, as the crust would bear them up.

On the ridge which formed the cove, deer paths were very plenty; and we had just reached the top of it when we came upon a drove of them.

They had no paths to run in except the ones we were travelling along. The unfortunate creatures were caught in a trap by being at one end of their yard, while by chance we had come between them and their only way out. The ground was covered with spruce and fir trees with branches high enough for us to look under for some distance. Thus we could see the frightened creatures wildly looking in all directions; they seemed to know that they could not escape through the untrodden snow, and also that that was their only chance.

It did not take them long to decide. Away they went, clearing the snow at every bound. But their strength was not sufficient to carry them far, and the sharp crust, through which they broke at each bound, cut their legs and breasts. They slackened their speed by the time they had gone twenty rods. As soon as we understood the trap they were in, we gave them chase; and our snow-shoes carrying us over the snow in a growth where there was no underbrush, gave us all the advantage.

It was not more than ten minutes before we were up with them. The poor creatures were so frightened that many of them uttered the most plaintive bleating, while a few of the older ones turned and gave us battle by jumping straight for us, with ears laid back, and wild-looking eyes, at the same time striking with their forefeet. But we still had all the advantage, for one step to the right or left let them bury themselves in the snow at our side; and it took them some time to get up, swing around, and strike again.

During all this time we were whooping and yelling at the top of our voices. Taking it all together, there was a curious noise: the bleating of the frightened deer, the snort and whistle of the furious buck as he made charge after charge, and all the noise we could make. It caused the mountains and valleys which usually sent back clear echoes, to do nothing but rumble and roar.

After the big bucks had jumped at us several times, they seemed to fear us less, and would stand beside us where they plunged in the snow for several minutes at a time before renewing the attack.

At one of those lulls in the conflict we decided that each of us would jump astride one and take a ride. We were about forty feet apart, and on the brow of the ridge where it pitched toward the Little Magalloway at a point where the descent is much more abrupt than the ascent from the Lake. At the signal we both mounted, and instantly found that we had no way of carrying our rifles, so they went into the snow under the deer's feet. The feet did not stop to trample upon them, but forced the deer and its rider into the air high enough to clear the snow, and with force enough to carry them about fifteen feet down the steep hill-side.

Where we struck, we found we had still more about us than we needed for such a ride; and that was our snow-shoes; they seemed to be particularly huge and unhandy things, but we had no time to unfasten them, as our hands were locked tight under the deer's necks, and unless we had ridden enough, it would not do to part them.

And doubtless we both thought it was no lynx affair, at least on our part, so we let the snow-shoes take care of themselves, and after the first bound they went behind and did not get under the deer again. Our ride was not long, yet it was exciting, and our minds were not upon any thing else; and after the performance was over, one could not laugh at the other, for he did not see him. About ten rods from where we mounted the deer was level ground; and once on that the mighty bucks were at our mercy. They tried several times to jump, but their strength was too far gone, and they could not clear the snow.

A Pair of Novel Steeds

As we lay on them, we could hear their hearts beat through their violent exertions. Then came the question, 'What was to be done with them?' and we agreed that when they got quiet we would let them go. It was not long before they gave up and sank into the snow completely conquered. When we got off they did not bounce away, but swinging their heads around, they gave us a look as much as to say. What next?

We left them and went back up the hill, picked up our hats, and dug up our rifles. We looked around to see if there were any more deer to ride back down the hill, but they all had got by us, and gone back into the yard. We then took our course again for Long Pond, very well satisfied with buck-riding for the season.

Chapter Twenty-Four - A Night in the Woods

AROUND the outlet we set several traps for mink, then walked up the Pond on the ice. When we were nearly to the inlet, we found a beaver house, and a good deal of wood in the water and on the ice, near where a spring brook made an opening. We had but one beaver trap with us. We set that where they came out of the water into the snow to cut their wood. Then we started along up the stream, but the alders and willows were so thick that we turned back and went to a point on the east side of the pond, where we sat on a log in the sun and ate our midday meal.

Then, as the snow was getting soft, we slowly walked toward home the way we came. When we got back as far as Fern Hill, we looked for our tamed bucks, but they were nowhere to' be seen; and their tracks told us where they had gone, which was back into the yard to join their comrades. We were obliged to wear our snow-shoes across the Lake, to keep our feet out of the water in the snow on the top of the ice. Long before we reached camp, we wished there was a buck going our way, as we should surely jump on.

The next day we went up Black Cat Brook, digging out and resetting traps.

Where we killed the caribou, the sable had been around; but the snow had prevented the traps from springing. We got some more caribou meat there, and took it to camp with us, where we spread it out over night to freeze, so we could bury it in the snow and keep it against a time of possible need.

We had not explored the valley of Moose Brook, so the next morning we took our knapsacks, with traps and our dinners, an axe, our rifles, and left camp at daylight. We followed up the river, and crossed the Lake to the place where we shot the buck in the fall; then put on our snow-6hoes and took an easterly course.

The thick bushes which are almost impossible to get through in summer, were bent down and held fast in the snow, so that we could walk over them without trouble. The snow had not melted enough to raise the streams, the dry snow underneath holding it like a sponge. After going about a mile from the Lake, we struck the stream, and found it so rapid that we could see the water nearly all the time as we went along.

The great accumulation of snow, thawed and settled by the sun, then frozen during the night, had made a sort of sidewalk, sometimes on one side, then on the other, as the stream changed its course. But we had no trouble in crossing, for every few rods big rocks held the ice from falling, and the snow on it made good bridges. We found after going about two miles that it made a sharp turn, and came straight from the north, and was more rapid for about half a mile. Then we came to a broad valley, where two streams joined; one coming from the east, but the larger one straight from the north. Just below where the two streams joined, and where the rapids began, the beaver had built a large, strong dam, which converted the valley above into a pond a mile long and nearly as wide. This was completely filled with alders and willows, which stuck up through the ice and snow, and so thick that it was impossible for us to go through with snow-shoes on, except where the main stream used to run. We followed along up its winding bed, and when nearly up to where the stream came tumbling in from the north, we found two very large beaver houses. Either of them would measure ten feet in diameter, and eight feet high. On the bank of the stream, just where it entered the pond, the beaver had recently cut a birch tree, thirteen inches in diameter, and the snow around the tree was covered with chips, some of them two inches across and half an inch thick.

From the birch to the water, which was about forty feet, there was a well-trodden path where they travelled to and from their work. It gave us an excellent chance to set a trap, and we did it. Although there were a large number of beavers in the family, we could find no other place where they came out; so we were obliged to leave without setting other traps.

We followed up the stream above the pond, but we could not go on it, because it was so narrow, and overhung with trees. We were obliged to take to the woods. Another mile and a half brought us to another level tract of country, much longer, but not so wide. There we also found beaver. They had done the usual thing — built a dam and overflowed the country. We did not go far up their pond, as it was getting late; but we set a trap in the sluice which they always have over the dam. Then we turned back toward the Lake.

Knowing we had travelled east, then north, for several miles, we knew we must hit the Lake if we took a southwest course, and would have less miles to travel; so we left the brook and started in that direction. After going about a mile we came to a little brook, where we built a fire and cooked some meat for dinner.

It was past noon, and the snow had become quite soft, and when we were ready to start again we found our snow-shoes would not keep us on the top of the snow. The softened crust would almost hold us, then give way and let Us down about two feet into the loose dry snow underneath. This made the travelling very hard and also very slow, and where it was up hill it was all we could do to get along. The afternoon was fast passing, and, unless we could reach the Lake before dark, we must sleep in the woods, for we had no tracks to follow, and after dark in the woods, under those circumstances, a man is nowhere. We fully realized our situation, and pushed on as fast as we could. At sunset we thought we must be near enough to the Lake to reach it before dark. We thought of nothing else, and hurried along; but night was soon upon us, and we had seen no signs of the Lake.

We were so sure that it could not be far off, we kept on for some time after it was so dark that we could not tell each other from the trunks of the trees. But at last we were obliged to give it up, and do the best we could.

Then we saw how foolish we had been not to have stopped before dark while we could have seen to cut wood for a fire. "But there was no use crying about spilt milk."

There *must* be a fire made, for we were wet to the skin. We first lit a match and looked around from tree to tree while its faint light lasted, trying to see a white birch tree, that we might get some bark; but we could not see any. Then we groped our way along a short distance, and looked again for white birch; at last we found the desired tree. It was the best-looking one we ever saw, although it was small. We got some bark from it, and soon had a torch which lit up the woods for rods around. We could, see several birch trees, and from each we got bark.

Then we began to look for a dry tree for wood. It did not take long to find that. Then one held the torch while the other cut wood until the one with the torch was cold. Then we would change. We worked so until we had wood enough to build a good fire.

Then with our snowshoes we scooped out a hole in the snow nearly to the ground, where we made our fire; and the light of that was all we wanted to cut more wood by. While one was cutting wood the other gathered boughs, and by midnight we were very comfortably fixed for camping. Our stomachs told us our suppers were wanted after so many hours of very hard work. We opened our knapsacks and found we had a very small piece of meat which was left from dinner. We divided it, eating very slowly, so as to make the meal good in one way; that was, in length of time.

After we had eaten our meat we laid down on our boughs and soon were fast asleep. But toward morning the fire got low, and the cold aroused us, for our clothes had not dried. We replenished the fire and attended to warming ourselves and drying our clothes, and before we were ready to lie down again daylight began to appear, and we were glad to see it. As soon as it was light enough to travel in the woods, we started. The walking was again good, the snow having frozen during the night so that it would bear us. We looked at the compass for west, and followed its directions; in less than fifteen minutes we came out to the Lake not far from the mouth of Moose Brook. Fifteen minutes more of daylight the evening before, and we could have reached the Lake. Once on it we could have gone to the home camp and saved that bad night in the woods.

We went directly to the camp, where we broke over the rules for the first time, by taking a good square meal of the best the camp afforded; and we really enjoyed it. We did not leave camp that day excepting to cut a little dry wood for kindling the fire. We spent the time in looking over our journal and talking over things that happened six months before — our ride on the steamer *Diamond* for one thing; and we thought we would like to meet the same crowd on our way out that we met coming in.

The snow had melted so much about our door that it looked as though spring had really come; but everywhere else through the woods it had a different appearance. Still the snow had really settled a good deal.

Chapter Twenty-Five - We Lose Our Hats

As we did not want to take our little boat down the river with us, knowing the large one would carry us and our load, we thought best to hide it where no parties would be likely to go during the summer. Then we should be sure of it the next fall. A short distance down the river, on the opposite side from the camp, was an irregular shaped ledge, about fifty feet high; and in some of the sheltered corners of that ledge we thought we should find a good place to lodge the boat.

So early in the morning, while the crust would bear us, we put the boat on the sled, and, with some trouble, worked it through the woods along the rapids, all the while looking for some ice bridge where we could cross. At last we saw one. It was not much wider than the sled, but looked solid. We tried it by pounding on it with a long pole, before we ventured on it ourselves. The water was not more than two feet deep under it, but it run with such force that it would be impossible for a man to stand in it for an instant. So we did not care to run any risks. After satisfying ourselves that it was safe, we drew our boat across, then along the bank of the river to the ledge, where we found an overhanging cliff with no snow under it. There we put the boat, laying it on two short logs so that it would not get out of shape, and covered it all over with boughs.

It had taken us some time to fix it, and the crust had nearly all gone when we were ready to go back. But we got along on our snow-shoes without much trouble, and making the best time we could, we walked on to the ice bridge, not thinking it had thawed enough to weaken it. But when we were near the centre it gave way, and we found ourselves in the current, and also in trouble which looked bad for us.

For the current caught our snow-shoes and instantly put us on our backs, with our heads under water. As instantly we were aware of the danger we were in, of being swept under the ice which was not more than ten rods below us.

We tried desperately for the shore. We gained a little, and when about half way to the ice, a friendly rock which came nearly to the surface, saved us. By chance one of us struck against it and clung to it, and the other was so near that he caught hold of the one on the rock.

Then with a great deal of trouble we got our snow-shoes off and threw them ashore, and after they were off we had no trouble reaching it ourselves, except from being stiff and nearly frozen, having been so long in the ice water.

But the greatest trouble came after we were on shore — getting in to camp. Our fingers were so numb and stiff that we could not tie on our snow-shoes, and.it was almost impossible to walk without them. Nor would it answer for us to stand still there in the snow, with our teeth chattering, as there was danger of breaking them. We tried to creep, but our hands would break through the snow, and in spite of ourselves, our faces would strike the snow. Our movements were not lively, and if we got a start in any direction, we could not help stumbling. At last we hit upon the right tiling, and that was to roll over and over till we got to camp. So stretching ourselves at full length on the snow, we began to roll. It caused a curious sensation, and nearly put us to sleep; but we were aware that we must not sleep there on the snow, so with a great deal of exertion, we kept awake. Every few feet we rolled against a tree, which caused a good deal of delay. At last we rolled into the path leading from the camp to the river where we got our water.

If anyone could have seen us as we were trying to walk along that path to the camp, they would have said, "Those fellows are either drunk or crazy."

Our trouble was not at an end on reaching camp; the fire was all out, and it took us a long time to light a match; our fingers being so stiff that we could not hold it — it would turn around and we would drop it. This happened several times before we got one to burn; and then it seemed as though a fire never burned so slowly before. As soon as it was well under way, we went out of camp, near the door where the snow was hard, and tried to dance; but our feet were too numb. Then we tried to run, but that hurt. At last we tried to wrestle, a thing we had never tried so long as we had been together. It was the best thing we could have done, because in a few minutes we got interested in it, and one was determined that the other should not throw him, and have it to tell of afterwards. The violent exercise in the warm sun soon brought the, blood to our fingers, and by the time the match was decided we were warmer than we had been for hours.

Then we went into camp, and beside the crackling fire we changed our clothes and agreed never to tell which was the best man.

The next morning we went back to find our sled, axe and hats. We found the sled about half a mile below the point where the bridge went down; it had gone under several places where the ice was from two feet to several rods in width, just as we would have gone, if the rock had not been placed there for us to support ourselves against until we could get our snowshoes off.

We rescued the sled without much trouble, by means of a long pole with a hook on the end of it. The axe and our hats we never found. The axe we could get along without, as we had one left at the camp; but our hats! We looked long and carefully for them, for they were all we had, and it seemed hard to part with them; but we were obliged to give lip the search, for the snow was getting soft.

It was necessary that we should have a substitute for a hat; but what should it be? We thought over the articles in our wardrobe, but could not hit upon any thing that would answer.

We finally gave up the idea of a brim, and began to look for something for a cap; but that, too, was no easy thing to find. We had plenty of skins, but we would rather go without any thing, than use one of them for any such purpose; our minds were set on selling all the skins, and we would not sacrifice one simply to cover our heads.

At last we hit on the very thing that would answer the purpose, which was to take one pair of our trousers — a pair that was badly worn — and cut off the legs at the knees. Then we took a section above, about eight Inches long, sewed up one end, turned up the other, to make it firmer, and there was a cap that answered every purpose.

Chapter Twenty-Six - Preparing to Move

THE weather was getting so warm that travelling in the woods, for only a few hours in the morning, was out of the question. So we thought best to confine our trapping to the Lake and river, where we could go to the traps and back before the morning crust was gone. Accordingly we made arrangements to get all the traps which we had up Moose Brook. We gathered a lot of birch bark, rolled it into tight bundles, about three inches in diameter, keeping them in shape by tying a string around them near one end. We then fastened twelve of those rolls to one of our knapsacks, after packing our dinners.

At twelve o'clock at night we left camp. We found no trouble in travelling on the river and Lake up to the point where we came on to the Lake the morning after we slept in the woods. There we lighted one of our rolls of bark, and hunted for the place where we camped. It took some time to find it, as the snow showed no tracks; but when we at last reached it, we had no trouble in following the tracks we had made in coming from Moose Brook to the camping ground. We could walk in the frozen track without snow-shoes. When one roll of bark had burned nearly to the hand, we would light another; so without any trouble we followed the old path to the spot where we ate our dinners on the way out. After that, it was more difficult, and at last we lost it.

We thought we must be near the Brook, and as it would be daylight in another hour, we made a fire in a dry stub and waited; and while waiting, we ate some of our dinner. As soon as we could see to travel, we took an easterly course and soon reached the stream a short distance below the beaver dam. We went there, and found we had a beaver in the trap, which we took out and skinned. Putting both skin and trap in the knapsack, we hurried along down to the other beaver pond, where we had another beaver, which we also skinned, and then pushed forward toward the Lake, following the Brook, which we reached before the sun had melted the snow to bother us much.

Just as we came out on to the Lake we saw an animal trotting along on the ice close under the trees, on a small island about half a mile distant. It was a curious-looking creature, and we watched it with considerable interest. It was near the south end, and when it reached the point it left the island and struck straight for Moose Brook point, about thirty rods from us. We stood perfectly still and watched it as it came across the Lake. We examined it very closely, as we had never before seen such an odd-looking creature; but in a few minutes we saw what it was.

It was our tailless fox!

We saw that he intended to go on the opposite side of the point from us, so we elevated our sights to forty rods and shot at him. Quick as a flash he changed ends and fairly flew across the Lake, disappearing in the woods on the west side.

We had a hearty laugh, and then resumed our journey toward camp, which we reached before noon. In the afternoon we stretched our beaver skins; then spread our blankets on the chips in the door-yard, and laid down and slept in the sun.

The next day we went to Long Pond, but we did not start as early as we did the day before, the distance not being more than one-half as far, and all we cared for was to reach the head of the cove by daylight; and this we did.

At the Pond we got one beaver and a mink; the beaver we skinned, but the mink we brought to camp with us, and also all the traps we had had there.

When we reached camp we were surprised to see the door standing wide open. We were startled, and hurried along as fast as we could to see who the intruders were, thinking all the time that some one had stolen our fur and gone.

But upon reaching the camp we found no one in or about it, and no tracks to show that any one had been there excepting ourselves. We came to the conclusion that. we must have left the door so that it came open of its own accord.

We had rushed up to camp in such a hurry that several little birds which were picking up crumbs near the door, flew in and darted about, nearly frightened to death; we caught them and put them outside, and our fur being all right, we were again happy.

The next morning we gathered in our traps up the Black Cat Brook, and found a sable in one of the traps where we shot the caribou. We saw that the snow was settling very fast, although the streams had not begun to rise. Trapping, where we must go through the woods, was at an end.

We thought to set a few traps along the river, but it was almost impossible to get there, so we abandoned that scheme. Knowing that we had our furs, a camp-kit, and the remaining provisions to take across the carry to the boat, we felt it was none too soon to begin treading a path.

We did not work on it until the snow was soft, so we made only a little way each day; but when it was finished, we could go over it in the morning without snow-shoes. This labor occupied us for several days, and all the time, the snow had been quietly settling; so we thought best to move at once to the Little Magalloway, and there wait for the river to clear itself of ice.

Early on the morning of April 10th, we started our first load, which consisted of a part of our camp-kit, the caribou and deer horns, a bag of spruce gum which we had gathered during the winter, our shelter tent and snowshoes. When we reached the boat, the first thing was to remove the snow so that we could have a place to pitch our tent. After we got the snow away we put up the tent, then took the logs which we had around our provisions under the boat, and of them built sides and back to our tent, so that we could have a comfortable place to sleep in when we were ready to live there. Our camp-kit, horns and gum we put under the boat.

When we returned to camp the walking was a little soft, but we got along very well on snowshoes.

Chapter Twenty-Seven - A Bear Hunt

THE next morning we started to draw across nearly all our provisions and all our caribou meat except enough for one more night. We had gone about a mile from camp when we saw in the snow that some animal had wallowed along, leaving a trail nearly three feet wide, and nearly reaching through to the ground. We were astonished at such a sight. We approached the track as cautiously as though we expected it would bite. When we got a fair look into it, we saw that it was the track of a bear, and a big one which the warm weather had awakened from his six months' sleep.

In less than five minutes we were hurrying back to camp with our load, thinking of nothing but a fight with a bear. We hastily put into our knapsacks provisions enough to last us until the next night, then taking axe and rifles, we started out again, not neglecting to take along cartridges enough to kill twenty bears.

We were not long in reaching the trail, where we put our snow-shoes on, and with ready rifles hurried along, to get as far as we could before the crust softened.

The bear had come from some hole along the river, and was striking across the country in a westerly course toward the Little Magulloway, which we knew could not be more than four miles ahead of us. We hoped to overhaul him before he crossed it. We knew the work he was doing must tire him fast, for it was no light work to make such a trail as that was through the damp snow. We also knew that the bear must have passed our road sometime after we went over it on our way to camp the night before, and also before it froze, as his track was left in the soft snow nearly in the centre of it. We had travelled nearly a mile on his trail, and found no signs of his being tired, or that he was there after it began to freeze.

The sun was getting well up, and the crust began to feel its effects. We went hurrying along as fast as we could, the perspiration streaming from every pore, determined to reach him before the crust gave out, if possible. The country over which we had travelled so far, had been nearly level, but just ahead of us we could see a hill, and were afraid that there might be a ledge in which he could hide himself. But upon reaching it we found there was none, but that the bear had made his bed under the roots of an upturned tree; and also that he had not left it until startled by our approach. Yet he was nowhere in sight, and we could see by his trail that he was getting out of that country as fast as his mighty power could force him along.

We had been hurrying all the morning; but such fresh signs caused us to nearly double our speed. The fast melting crust would give way under our snow-shoes every few minutes, causing us to go headlong into the snow. Then we would scramble up and rush on again, each trying to keep a little in advance of the other.

Climbing the hill, although it was short work, nearly took away our breath; but in going down the other side, where the sun had not softened the crust, we regained it, and there we could run without any danger of breaking through. But the bear found it still more difficult to perform his part in the race for his life, for the crust would not hold him, and his speed continually slackened, and soon we were in view of him.

We welcomed the sight with loud yells, and rushed along to make him show his bringing up; a thing he was perfectly willing to do, although he was in too much snow to amount to much as a fighter.

When he saw there was no chance to escape, he turned and faced us, giving a fierce growl.

We could have shot him then, but we had worked too hard not to have a little fun with him. All we were afraid of was that he would take a back track. We agreed that if he attempted to do this we would bore him at once.

We walked up to within about thirty feet of him. He never moved, but sat up, lolling like a dog after a hard run. There did not seem to be much fight in him, and to awaken his dormant ideas, we threw clubs at his head. At first he seemed to take that as a joke; but when one about two feet long and three inches in diameter, struck him square across the nose, he rallied, and it surprised us a good deal to see how quickly he reached the place where we were standing. Only our snow-shoes carried us beyond his reach.

After a second attempt to hug us he gave it up, and started for his winter abode. We saw his game, and opened fire on him. It was wonderful how he could stand the lead, and for a time we thought we were going to lose him. At last his body began to quiver, and presently he sank in the snow to rise no more.

It was the largest black bear we had ever seen, and we knew he must be very fat, as he had just come from his six months' rest; therefore we let him lay and cool while we made arrangements for putting in the night, as we knew it would be impossible for us to reach the home camp before dark. After eating our dinners we cleared away the snow and built a bough-camp and cut wood for the night; then we were ready to commence on the bear. Near where he lay we dug the snow away, then rolled him into the cleared place so that we could have a good chance to work. It was a great task to get his skin off, and not leave it covered with fat; but at last it was done, and we began to cut off the coating of fat encasing his back and sides. It was about two inches thick. Then we opened him, taking the fat from the inside, putting all of it into a birch-bark box which we made for the purpose.

By the time the job was done, night was upon us. We picked some boughs for a bed, spread our bear skin on them, making a good couch, where, before a cheerful fire, we spent one of the pleasantest evenings of the winter.

The next morning the fat in the box was quite stiff and hard, so we rolled our bear skin around it and fastened it to two poles, and carried it between us on our shoulders to our road, then went for the sled, on which we drew it to camp. The rest of the day we spent in getting out the oil, which we put in the can we had brought molasses in. We did not stretch the skin, as it would take some time for it to dry; and we could wait until we got moved to our quarters on the Little Magalloway.

Chapter Twenty-Eight - Farewell to the Home Camp

THE second morning after this we were again ready to leave the home camp, having hidden all our traps, and taken across the carry all but one load, which consisted of furs and blankets, and was safely on the sled. Before we left, we put a sign over the door. It read:

May all parties who visit this camp have as pleasant a time as we have had,
Barker and Danforth.
April 14th, 1877.

The big load of furs and blankets bothered us a good deal in crossing the carry; not on account of its weight, but of its bulk, as it was wider than the road in many places. But we got it over at last, and then we were ready for the ice in the river to break up.

Our stock of provisions was not gone. We had been very careful to not eat more than our allotted rations, having broken the rules but once. We stretched our bear skin between two trees, and amused ourselves for a day or two in using up our cartridges on a target. But it was dull music to lay around camp day after day with nothing to do except to shoot at a target. Still we were obliged to do it for nearly a week.

At last the weather which had been fine for so long a time, with clear warm days and cold nights, grew warmer, so that the crust did not last more than an hour or two in the morning; the sky gradually grew hazy, and the sun as it sank behind the mountains left a gray gloom behind as a twilight; and finally the morning came without any crust, and the sun was not to be seen.

Heavy clouds which hung low spread a gloom over the country which was almost appalling. A thick fog rose from the valleys and hid even the nearest hills from view. Soon the ruin began to fall, not in torrents, but in gentle showers; not a breath of air disturbed its quiet descent. Still the snow seemed to melt before its touch.

The small mountain streams began to perform their duties once more, and in a few hours could be heard roaring through the deep woods. The larger streams in the valleys passed the water along to swell the river which carried the winter mantle of the Upper Malloway to the sea.

We sat on a log in front of our tent, with a rubber blanket over our shoulders, watching how gradually the water in the river crept up, inch by inch, forcing the ice from the banks until, after trembling for a minute, it rolled under with a swash, rose a few rods below, and then quietly sailed away. Ice that it had taken months to form, was gone in a few hours, so sudden was the change. But we were glad to see it; and the next day we made all arrangements for our departure, though we knew it would take several days for the ice to get out of the river. Of course we did not intend to start so as to get caught in a jam and have our boat smashed.

We had made up our minds to evade the questions if put directly to us by the Magalloway settlers when we got there, about the game north of Parmachenee Lake, and how much fur we had; we did not want them to think of going there to trap the next winter. To get our furs through the settlement, we packed them into four bundles as small as we could make them, and then sewed a blanket around each bundle. Such bundles we thought they would not notice thrown in among our camp kit. The overhauling of the fur and sewing it up occupied us for nearly one day.

During the following night we were aroused from sleep by a tremendous roaring. We raised up in bed and listened. The noise came from the north, and gradually grew louder and nearer. Soon we knew what it was; the water had filled the Lake, and now was coming on, pouring over the rapids; this had started the ice, and that now was also coming in a body, rolling and tumbling. We wished it was daylight, so we could go over to the main stream to see it pass; we thought we might, perhaps, see our old hats once more.

The rumbling kept coming nearer and nearer, until we could hear the crashing of timber as it plowed through the woods where the banks were low. At last it was opposite us; then it soon died away. Occasionally during the rest of the night, we could hear the swash of sections of the ice which had formed on the banks, as they gave way and fell into the water.

In the morning we went across to the main river. There we saw two banks of smashed ice, about eight feet high, with a boiling, seething stream rushing between them. It seemed as though the river must be clear for some distance. But we well knew that the dead part of the river could not yet be broken up. We thought it best to wait another day; and we contented ourselves as best we could.

But the next day we could stand it no longer; the storm was past, and the sun came out warm and bright. We launched our boat, and in a short time were all ready to start. On one of the poles which had supported the tent we put a sign which read:

A long winter of hard work has ended here, with eight days of quiet rest.
Barker and Danforth

Chapter Twenty-Nine - Return to Civilization

THEN we shoved our boat into the roaring river. Away we flew toward home and friends. Never did two fellows feel better than we did. We talked, laughed, sang and shouted while our boat parted the white-topped waves, skimming over the rapids below.

But toward night we sung a different song, as we found the low lands of the Magalloway all overflowed and the ice in the river nearly as solid as ever. And it was with a great deal of trouble that we pushed our boat through the alders and slush for nearly a mile, to get to ground that was out of water. Then we went into camp again, to wait for the sun and current to wear the ice out of our way.

The time did not hang as heavily on our hands, however, as it did before, for we amused ourselves shooting musk-rats. The overflow had forced them from their homes, and they had taken refuge on floating logs and stumps which lay scattered through the alders that covered the whole valley. Every morning and evening we climbed a tall spruce tree that grew near our tent, and looked out over the flooded country.

We could see the course of the river, marked by a strip of ice which had risen with the water.

On the fourth morning we started again, although the ice still hung in the river; but we could work along the edge of it and through the bushes. We were now obliged to try for home, for our meat was all gone, and our imported goods very short. All day we worked our boat along, sometimes drawing it over the ice, but most of the time forcing it along the edge and through the bushes.

At night we went ashore on a high knoll about half a mile from the river. Here we stayed the next day, and also ate our first musk-rat. And the only objection we could find to it was, that it was a rat; it tasted well enough, and we were glad it did, for in a day or two more we should be obliged to live on them.

We knew we could not catch them after we got below the meadows. So we stayed over another day and hunted musk-rats. When we got back to camp at night we found we had sixteen. We carefully dressed them, then strung them on a stick by passing it through their bodies, one after another, and hung them on the limb of a tree, so that we could cut from them such parts as might be tempting to our appetites.

The next morning before starting on our journey again, we made our breakfast almost entirely of rats' legs, fried in pork-fat; and they were really delicious.

We found the ice fast wasting away, so we did not have much trouble in getting along. But night again forced us to hunt for high ground, where we again pitched our tent and lived on musk-rats.

At daylight the next morning we were again forcing our boat among the alders; but in a few hours we got to that part of the river where the banks are higher and covered with forest trees. Here we found the current a great deal stronger, also less ice, so that in many places the river was clear for a mile in a stretch. That night we camped at the narrows, on the same ground where we camped when we went up the river. And the next night we jumped ashore at the head of Aziscoos Falls, and threw our pant-leg caps high in the air.

But it was too late for us to cross the carry. We pitched our tent once more. In the morning we did not stop for our breakfast of musk-rats, but started across the carry to the settlement where we got a good square, clean meal of victuals.

There was a little snow on the carry, but all the fields in the settlement were bare; and we learned from one of the farmers that the river was clear of ice below, and that the steamer *Diamond* was making weekly trips, and running to Brown's Farm, on account of the high water. We also found that this was the day for her to make a trip; so we determined to catch it if we could, in order to pass the settlement without letting very many of its people see our bundles of fur.

We at once engaged a farmer to take our boat over the carry and put it into the river at the foot of the Falls; from that point we would row to the steamboat landing. Before noon we had our boat and load on the river below the Falls; then we bent to the oars. We got in sight of the steamer just as she was swinging from the landing. We swung our pant-leg caps, and the captain let the boat drift until we overtook it and got on board. We had eaten no dinner, but we didn't care for that, as we had caught the steamer.

There were quite a number on board who greeted us gaily: "Well, boys, who cut your hair?" "How often do you shave?" "Who mended your clothes?" "Where do you buy your caps?" Many other such questions, too, there were, which we did not deign to answer.

That night we engaged a room at the Errol Dam Hotel, at Errol, N. H., where we packed all our fur in a big box. We shipped it from that point to a Boston firm.

The next morning as we separated for the summer, we shook hands and said we have had a good time, and, "Remember the coming fall!"

In a few days a letter enclosing the following bill, and a draft on the First National Bank of Boston, came to Errol; it was directed thus:

Pearl St., Boston, May 28th, 1877.

MESSRS. ————————,

SHIPPERS OF RAW FUR,

Bought of BARKER & DANFORTH,

"Barker & Danforth,

"Hunters and Trappers."

22	Mink, prime,	dark,	*at*	5.00	$110.00
7	" "	light,	"	3.50	24.50
4	Otter, prime,	dark,	"	10.00	40.00
5	" small,	light,	"	7.25	36.25
8	Fisher,	dark,	"	9.00	72.00
7	"	light,	"	6.50	45.50
1	Bear,	small,			7.00
1	"	spring, large, and black,			12.00
1	Red Fox,				2.25
65	lbs. Beaver,		"	2.00	130.00
104	Musk-rats,	fall,	"	.10	10.40
48	"	spring,	"	.15	7.20
6	Lynx,		"	3.00	18.00
34	Martens,	dark,	"	2.50	85.00
15	"	light,	"	1.90	28.50

$ 628.60

www.ingramcontent.com/pod-product-compliance
Lightning Source LLC
Chambersburg PA
CBHW032021040426
42448CB00006B/697